D0518735

THE PERFECT SCHOOL GOVERNOR

ofsted

Tim Bartlett Edited by Jackie Beere

 Independent Thinking Press

First published by
Independent Thinking Press
Crown Buildings, Bancyfelin, Carmarthen, Wales, SA33 5ND, UK
www.independentthinkingpress.com

Independent Thinking Press is an imprint of Crown House Publishing Ltd.

© Tim Bartlett 2013

British Library Cataloguing-in-Publication Data
A catalogue entry for this book is available
from the British Library.

Print ISBN 978-1-78135-090-4
Mobi ISBN 978-1-78135-094-2
ePub ISBN 978-1-78135-095-9

Printed and bound in the UK by
Gomer Press, Llandysul, Ceredigion

To my perfect daughter

Contents

Contents

Acknowledgements

Many people have generously contributed ideas, sample documents and time: time to talk with me, to read drafts and to make comments. I thank them all; and, of course, any errors are mine. John Beasley provided the learning walk in science and Matt Lynch provided the reasons for including policy review in the book. If you spot something you know I should have given you credit for, please forgive me – and let me know! The truth is I'm a magpie: as a school governor, I have collected brilliant things over the last 24 years and I use them to help make our schools even better places for our children and young people. Here they all are ...

Government policy and legislation, as far as we understand them, are correct up to 31 March 2013. It has been possible to make some small amendments during the final stages of production.

Foreword

It has never been more important to attract as governors people who can add value to schools. Having worked as a governor myself, and worked with governors as a head teacher, I know that they can be a support or an irritation, an inspiration or an obstacle to the success of a school. Governors need to rise above the everyday concerns and ask the big questions about strategy and results. They need to be confident enough to raise issues with the head teacher and to engage with staff and children during school contact time. They need to know how to work as a team of professionals who believe in a set of shared values that will deliver the shared vision for a successful school. All of this, for no financial reward – as yet – and a huge quantity of paperwork and procedures to wade through at every meeting. Make no mistake, this is a demanding role, but also an immensely satisfying contribution to any community.

Some governors will come to their first meeting having no more knowledge of the world of education than their own schooling and perhaps the gossip from the school gate or horror stories from their children. How empowering to have the chance to see beyond this into the complex world of school improvement! Governors begin to realise how staffing decisions are made, school budgets are spent and feel the pressure of school accountability when Ofsted arrives.

The days of governors meeting once or twice a term and making the occasional appearance at the school show are over. Now governors are held responsible, as part of the school leadership, during inspection. They are expected to know how well the school is performing and show that they know what is being done to improve it. This requires governors to be able to observe lessons, understand complex performance data and contribute to school development plans.

Governors give their time, their expertise and, crucially, a different perspective to the challenges schools face, ensuring, together with the school leadership, that our schools work hard for every child. In many areas, local authorities no longer play a central role in monitoring and improving schools and academies, so it is even more important that governance can provide the support and challenge that delivers a high quality education. This is a huge expectation and a learning journey for everyone who joins a governing body. Governors who have an open mind, a mission to understand and who are open to learn are the very best assets that a head teacher can have to help deliver outstanding outcomes for children.

What governors need in order to do all this successfully is a practical, readable, handy guide with all the crucial information to hand, which they can dip into and learn from as needed. Tim, with all his wealth of experience to draw upon, has produced that guide in this little book. Its strengths are in its attention to detail, readability and useful resources – and in the confidence it will give governors to do a brilliant job for their school community.

Jackie Beere, Tiffield

Introduction

We become governors with various levels of knowledge and many different experiences – that's part of the value of governing bodies. It is a vital job and someone has to do it! It is also a *powerful* job, as the purpose of a governing body is to challenge and support the leadership of your school (yes, *your* school, now). The aim of this book is to help you become the very best governor you can be.

This Introduction includes a quick-start guide as an overview of the governor's role – this chapter is chiefly aimed at first-time governors. This is followed by six chapters which are aimed at all governors who wish to demonstrate best practice. Each begins with a brief summary which allows you to gain an overview to select your priority areas for more detailed reading.

Quick-start guide

This section provides:

■ An introduction to educational jargon and acronyms

■ Advice on how to approach your first meeting as a governor

Terms used in the book

Throughout this book I have used the following terms: *governor*, *governing body*, *head teacher*, *school*, *parent*, *pupil* and *student*. This is to make reading this book as simple as possible and because these seemingly straightforward words hide all sorts of complexities, as explained below.

Governor covers an increasing range of different titles used in schools, such as trustee, board member, local governor, company director, member of an interim executive board. The vast majority of governors gift their time and expertise to the school.

Governing body similarly covers a group of governors who have, between them, a wide range of expertise. What governing bodies all have in common is that they are responsible for the school over the long-term and for ensuring that the school provides the highest possible standards of education. They are part of the formal organisation of the school and offer support and challenge to the staff. This book empha-sises this role of support and challenge.

The **head teacher** may be called a principal, proprietor, executive head, chief executive, high master or head mistress.

School covers many different types of organisation – it might be an academy, specialist college, university technology col-lege or an independent, community, foundation, free or studio school. What they all have in common is that they exist to educate children, usually called **pupils** in primary schools or **students** in secondary schools.

Parents covers foster parents, parents who live apart from each other, step-parents, carers or even a local authority. They all have a legal duty to educate the children in their care.

Jargon busting

If education terminology is new to you, then take this book with you, especially to your first meeting. A photocopy of the jargon-buster pages may be unobtrusive – or use your tablet computer if you have one. Laptops have largely failed to gain a foothold in meetings – the screen seems to act as a physi-cal barrier – and if you keep looking at your smartphone your colleagues might think you are texting for someone to come and rescue you!

Firstly, here is some information about the different types of school. If nothing else, reading this section will persuade you that the education system in England is very varied. A word of warning: you are about to be served quite a large bowl of alphabet soup.

Jargon-buster 1: School funding arrangements

One key difference between schools is their funding source. **Private schools** charge fees. **State schools** do not charge fees. They are *publicly funded* by one of the following bodies:

- The Education Funding Agency (EFA), which is an agency of the Department for Education (DfE).
- The local authority where they are located. In a county council area that will be the local authority; elsewhere, it will be the unitary authority.

State schools can be referred to as independent schools in that they are independent of control by a local authority. More usually, however, the term 'independent school' is used to mean a private school.

Jargon-buster 2: Different types of school

Academy. An independent state school and always funded by the EFA. Academies are schools for pupils of all abilities. Secondary academies can opt to have a specialism and select up to 10% of their pupils who must show an aptitude for that speciality. The specialisms are: physical education or sports, performing arts, visual arts, modern foreign languages, design and technology and information technology.

Academies can be self-standing or operate as part of an academy chain.

In general, *all* state schools that are not community/maintained schools are academies, even if that is not in their name. Schools that that are not academies and that 'fail' an Ofsted inspection must close and reopen as a sponsored academy; that is, join a DfE-approved external organisation that will promote rapid improvement.

Academy chain. These are groups of academies with an overarching organisation which has a contract with the DfE. These organisations, which are not-for-profit charitable trusts, charge their member schools a maximum of 5% of their budget to provide services and leadership. Chains vary in how they establish governing bodies for individual schools and how they delegate authority to them.

Community/maintained school. A state school that is usually owned and always funded (maintained) by the local authority.

Free school. A state independent school set up in response to a request from the local community.

Grammar school. State secondary school which selects its pupils by means of an examination taken at age 11. There were 164 grammar schools in England and a further 69 in Northern Ireland at the time of writing.

High school. A secondary school that can be an alternative state school in areas where there are grammar schools, a state school that precedes an upper school (14–18-year-olds), or a private school.

Lower/first school. Part of the three-tier school system. These schools take children aged from 5–8 or sometimes 5–9.

Middle school. Part of the three-tier school system. These schools take children aged from 8–12 (i.e. primary) or children aged 9–13 or 10–13 (i.e. secondary). Pupils transfer from middle to upper or high schools.

Nursery school. State funded service for children over 3. Private voluntary or independent (PVI) nursery education is also available throughout the UK and varies between structured pre-school education and services offering child-minding facilities.

Preparatory school. Private primary schools, often abbreviated to 'prep' schools. Pupils are usually preparing for transfer to private secondary schools at age 11, 13 or 14.

Primary school. State school for children aged 5–11. These are sometimes split into reception (ages 4–5), infant (ages 5–7) and junior (ages 7–11).

Pupil referral unit. PRUs provide education for pupils who have been excluded (expelled) from a mainstream school or who are unable to attend a mainstream school for some other reason, such as ill health. PRUs can be academies, private or community schools.

Special school. These provide for pupils with special educational needs (SEN) and may be academies, private or community schools

Studio school. A state independent school for 14–19-year-olds of all abilities. The curriculum is designed to integrate the world of work closely into the pupils' learning activities and will admit up to 400 pupils. The unique element is the focus on enquiry-based learning. Often the students' two workplace specialisms are determined by the local economy (e.g. aeronautics, engineering, health, social care, tourism).

University technology college. UTCs are state independent schools for 14–19-year-olds of all abilities, run by a partnership between further education colleges and universities. They can admit up to 800 students and have at least two specialisms (e.g. engineering, construction, event management, environmental services) which are geared towards the skills needed for the local economy.

Upper/high school. Part of the three-tier school system These schools take children aged from 13–18 or 14–18.

Jargon-buster 3: High-frequency terminology for your first meeting[1]

AST. Advanced skills teacher – a senior member of staff, externally assessed for promotion on the basis of their teaching ability.

Cover supervisor. A member of staff who supervises a class when their regular teacher is absent. Teaching staff can only be required to cover for each other's absence in exceptional circumstances.

CPD. Continuing professional development – the school's training programme.

EYFS. Early Years Foundation Stage (ages 0–5).

HLTA. Higher level teaching assistant.

HMI. One of Her Majesty's Inspectors, a small group of independent school inspectors who now work for Ofsted.

HMCI. Her Majesty's Chief Inspector or the head of Ofsted.

Key Stage 1 (KS1). Years 1 and 2 (ages 5–7).

Key Stage 2 (KS2). Years 3–6 (ages 7–11).

Key Stage 3 (KS3). Years 7–9 (ages 11–14).

Key Stage 4 (KS4). Years 10 and 11 (ages 14–16).

LSA. Learning support assistant – works with a teacher in the classroom.

Ofsted. National inspection organisation covering all providers of services for children and young people – from Early Years to adults up to the age of 25 with special needs.

PPA time. Planning, preparation and assessment – teachers are guaranteed no less than 10% of the time they are scheduled to teach pupils to use for PPA and cannot be called on during this time except in emergencies.

QTS. Qualified teacher status.

SDP. School development plan – usually covers priorities for the next three years.

SEF. Self-evaluation form – an internal, objective assessment (usually using the same criteria applied in school inspections) in a format the school chooses to meet its own needs.

SLT. School/senior leadership team.

Support staff. School staff other than teachers.

TA. Teaching or teacher assistant.

Schools today: the governing body

A governing body is a critically important 'middle tier' – filling the vacuum between schools and national government This vacuum is the result of the accelerating dispersal of the previous powers and duties of local authorities to schools and national government.

Fortunately, their key legal responsibility can be summarised in a nutshell: 'The governing body has general responsibility for the conduct of the school with a view to promoting high standards of educational achievement.'[2]

The 2012 version of the Department for Education's *Governors' Guide to the Law* ran to 210 pages.[3] This list from the table of contents is worth reading because it really does give a complete overview of the areas of responsibility of governing bodies:

- Academy conversion
- The Early Years Foundation Stage and the national curriculum
- Children with special educational needs and other vulnerable children
- The school budget
- School premises and capital investment
- Staffing
- School improvement partners and school self-evaluation
- Admissions
- Behaviour and attendance
- Inspection
- Schools causing concern
- Health, safety and welfare
- Equalities
- Organisational changes to the school
- Trust schools
- Parent councils
- Control and community use of school premises
- Extended activities in schools
- Charging for school activities
- Providing information

Sometimes these responsibilities are shared between a school's governing body and one which is responsible for a group of schools. The DfE's 2013 version is much shorter.

Ofsted

Ofsted inspections focus on five areas:

1. Overall effectiveness

2. Achievement of pupils at the school

3. Quality of teaching in the school

4. Behaviour and safety of pupils at the school

5. Quality of leadership in, and management of, the school (including governance)

Ofsted grades each area separately as either:

1. Outstanding

2. Good

3. Requires improvement

4. Inadequate

A grade 3 school will be monitored by Ofsted, including further visits to the school. A school with an overall grade of 4 will be judged either to have 'serious weaknesses' or to require 'special measures'. Each of these brings a higher level of monitoring, support and intervention to ensure rapid improvement. Schools with either of these judgements are often referred to as being 'in an Ofsted category'.

Your first governors' meeting

Joining any team is a challenge. Even if the context is familiar, the relationships and ways of working together vary between different groups, plus the use of language can be baffling. You know that what you are hearing is in English but you can only vaguely recognise the meaning!

It is unlikely that the chair will ask you to express a view at your first meeting without having a word with you beforehand. However, expect to be invited to introduce yourself, so prepare a sentence or two on how you became a governor and what you hope to contribute.

The next problem is that the agenda for the meeting is 'work in progress' – a combination of what went before and what is to come. Agendas are full and time is short: you are leaping onto a roller-coaster. This can be exciting but also daunting, so the best advice is to cling on and try to enjoy the ride. There will be moments when the pace slows and you will just be feeling you've got the hang of an item on, for example, providing additional activities at lunchtime; and there will be times when you will be over the top and hurtling down with an item on comparing year-on-year data on attainment. Having just worked out what attainment means, the words *progress, achievement, floor targets* and *benchmark* will fly by in a blur. Just hang on! Jot down the terms you're unfamiliar with and, if you've not already been allocated a mentor – a governor to call your own – now is the time to make a note to ask the chair of governors for a suggestion.

Who's who?

A full governing body meeting will include the *chair of governors*, *vice chair*, *head teacher*, *clerk* and the other governors – some of whom will have specific roles, for example, *chair of the finance committee*. There might also be *observers* present – members of the leadership team and other staff may be invited for all of the agenda or to join the meeting for a particular matter.

The *clerk to the governor*s is almost always paid for the time they give and will be able to advise the governing body on legal and procedural issues. They are responsible for recording the meeting and preparing minutes from their notes.

What matters is that all governors are equal and act *together* to discharge their legal responsibilities. The chair of governors and chairs of committees will exercise some authority and have a closer working relationship with the head teacher than other governors. That authority is granted by the governing body, not by the position. The governing body may also delegate functions to an individual.

Pamela Hutchison, head teacher of Elizabeth Woodville School, Northamptonshire, provides these top tips for governors:

1. Get to know the school during the day – two half-day visits.

2. You will find the first few meetings difficult – that's a fact. There's a lot to learn and too little time, always.

3. You volunteer *once*, then you are committed. You have signed up to being a governor and *all* that it entails.

4. Always be aware that just because *you* don't know about something, this doesn't mean it isn't happening. Ask questions accordingly.

5. Governing bodies should schedule all meetings as far ahead as possible.

6. We are all trying to be honest – sharing the positives in the journey we are on. Be open to debate.

7. Listen out for persuasive arguments – even just two governors may be right.

Safety

If you are already a school governor then, under the current provisions for safeguarding children, you may already have been asked to provide what was known as an enhanced CRB (Criminal Records Bureau) check, now a DBS (Disclosure and Barring Service) check. If you are thinking about becoming a governor, then be prepared for this. Although it is unlikely that in the course of undertaking the role you will have regular unsupervised access to children, the clerk to the governing body can request that you undergo a check. Failure to comply with such a request is grounds for disqualification as a governor.

This is enough to get you started. Good luck!

Chapter 1

Strategic leadership and how governors provide it

This chapter will:

▒ Cover what strategic leadership means and how governors can provide leadership in their schools

▒ Describes governors' meetings and how to get the best out of them

▒ Offer advice about how to find out if you are achieving what you set out to achieve

Long-term leadership

The literature often refers to the governing body's 'strategic role' but most of us are lost amongst the subtle differences between a strategy, a plan, a policy and a framework.

School staff will come and go but the governing body remains. It is this difference that highlights its main function.

Governors take the longer strategic view: assessing where we are now as a school, agreeing on where we are going, finding out whether we are on track and what needs to be done to improve the quality of education.

The focus must always be on sustaining quality teaching, and learning what has a positive impact on pupils' progress at the school, especially those who are at risk of underachieving.

> Inspection examines the impact of all leaders, including those responsible for governance, and evaluates how efficiently and effectively the school is managed. In particular, inspection focuses on how effectively leadership and management at all levels promote improved teaching, as judged within the context of the school, and enable all pupils to overcome specific barriers to learning, for example through the effective use of the pupil premium.[4]

The special challenges of governing body meetings

Schools are complex and there is always a mass of interesting detail to deal with. Lots of people want the governing body's attention so this needs to be carefully managed. Here is an example of the type of issue considered by a governing body: policy.

Policies

All organisations need policies – and education laws require schools to have policies of various kinds. In addition, other legislation, such as employment law, applies to schools. A school can decide if it wants to adopt a policy that no other school has in place. For example, federations and academy chains may decide they want additional common policies to make their partnership distinctive, such as on school uniform.

For the school year 2012/13, one academy in Nottingham had 48 current policies and the list noted that three more were needed – 51 in total. More than half, in April 2012, were overdue for updating. A figure of 51 is a typical number in most schools.

All policies need to be reviewed from time to time, so at the rate of reviewing each policy every three years, that means 17 per year or one every 11 school days. How to keep policies up to date is a key operational decision because it can take a lot of time. At the other extreme, some policies are just nodded through and take no time at all.

Policies are very important, so Chapter 2 deals with them in detail.

Effective meetings: fulfilling leadership and governance functions

All governing bodies have the responsibility for deciding how they will organise themselves. Exactly what they need to achieve will vary from school to school: the full range of functions for the governing body of a community school are summarised in the list on page 10; in independent schools (state or private) it will vary depending on the governance regime – the school may be self-standing or part of a group of schools.

Typically, the full governing body will meet five or six times per year as well as delegating functions like policy review to committees. At the start of each year, the governing body will decide the structure for the coming year. So, the governors of a self-standing school will confirm what committees it needs, who will serve on them and what their remits will be. There is not always complete freedom to choose, because a local authority or academy chain may issue guidance which should normally be followed.

The head teacher, clerk to the governors and chair of governors will decide what items will be on the agenda for governors' meetings, taking account of all the requirements, advice, previous experience and requests. Not surprisingly, the task of keeping a meeting running to schedule is no easier in a governing body than anywhere else, and the chair has an active part to play.

Chapter 1

Purpose of meetings

Many of us spend so much time in meetings that we some-times forget to ask ourselves and others why, exactly, are we all here? The answer divides into two parts – hard outcomes and soft outcomes.

1. Hard outcomes are:

    a. Agreements reached

    b. Decisions taken

    c. Solutions created

    d. Appropriate facts, views and evidence for judgements learned

Every agenda item needs to have one of these outcomes: it is one of the purposes of the chair to make clear at the start of the agenda item what the planned outcome is.

2. Soft outcomes are:

    a. Enhanced teamworking in order to better achieve the hard outcomes

    b. All present leave the meeting feeling satisfied that they have made a contribution to improving the quality of provision for pupils

    c. Increased commitment to the values that drive the school towards achieving its aims

    d. Enjoyment of each other's company

e. The staff present feel confidence in the ability of the governing body to contribute powerfully to the leadership of the school

---

Tip ☑

The chair should evaluate the governing body's hard and soft outcomes from time to time. Give everyone a sticky note, put a sheet of flipchart paper by the exit and ask everyone to rate the meeting with a number on their sticky note.

- 1 = Outstanding
- 2 = Good
- 3 = Requires improvement
- 4 = Inadequate

For example: *To what extent do you feel we are making a contribution to the quality of provision for pupils at our meetings?*

If action is needed, design and implement it, then repeat the evaluation to measure the distance travelled.

To evaluate staff confidence, invite the head teacher to consult with the staff and feed back to the chair.

Planning the meeting agenda

One local authority sends out a useful document at the start of each term which details all the items that governing bodies *might* consider putting on their agenda for the term. The headings are:

- Item
- Sources of supporting information
- List of contacts for further information or advice

The 2012 autumn term document runs to 14 pages!

Any group of schools with a central body will need this same sort of guidance – it is not just a local authority practice.

Tim Read, chair of governors at Elizabeth Woodville School, Northamptonshire provides his top tips for chairs of governors:

1. Agree your value base and the strategic framework within which you are taking decisions – a combination of the vision and how you are achieving it. Print them on something the size of a credit card. In that way, when a governor hasn't had time to read the paperwork before a meeting, they have something to relate to the discussion.

Contd

---

2. Build a team around you (e.g. chairs of committees) and go through the data, look at the curriculum and review governing body processes.

3. Maintain objectivity.

4. Everyone thinks they don't have power to get things done; but if you have confidence and clarity about what you want to achieve, everything will fall in behind it.

Scheduling and duration

In many schools, full governing bodies and committees meet on weekday evenings and with school staff present, either as governors or observers or to contribute to an agenda item. Many governors are in paid employment and have family responsibilities so daytime meetings involve taking time away from the workplace or home for all concerned.

However, evening meetings may be difficult for parents, carers and those who depend on public transport. For those working daytime hours, including school staff, evening meetings make for a very long working day.

Deciding when to meet is important but can be a source of conflict. The key difficulty is that the people present discussing the change of time are meeting at a time that is convenient to them. An alteration might mean that they will no longer be able to serve as a governor.

Whenever they take place, meetings need to be as short as possible and consistent with achieving their purpose. Schools usually work on the basis that meetings with and for staff should last no longer than one hour.

Governing bodies often set two hours as a limit. This may seem impossibly brief given the amount of responsibility a governing body has, but it is achieved by ensuring that the agenda contains only those items that the full governing body needs to consider. Everything else is delegated to a committee. This is how governing bodies fulfil their strategic leadership function.

Recording meetings

All meetings should be recorded. This is increasingly important as schools become more autonomous and have to account for everything they do – either to Ofsted or other external auditors.

Tip ☑

Develop a framework for recording the minimum information for committee and other smaller meetings.

Any framework for documenting meetings needs to be easy to use so that the person filling it in can also join in the meeting. Time taken over the formalities, like matters arising, should be as brief as possible. The meeting should focus on the reporting by individuals on actions they agreed to implement at the previous meeting, rather than just taking more comments on an item from the previous meeting's minutes.

You'll find an example in Appendix 3.

Tip ✓

Any other business (AOB) is usually placed at the end of the meeting. But, just when everyone is thinking of going home, up pops an item that someone insists is discussed.

To offset this problem, require anyone with an item of other business to declare it at the start of the meeting. This enables the chair to decide whether to adjust the agenda because this item is urgent enough to cover at this meeting, delegate it to a committee, make a note or postpone it to the next meeting.

Agreeing what needs to be done

The head teacher will agree the vision for the school along with the full governing body. Governors keep this objective in mind and then ask the right questions to check the school's progress towards achieving it. Setting the vision is not easy because a vision statement has to be straightforward, command the support of the whole school community and be distinguishable from that of every other school.

Primarily the head teacher and leadership team will be driving forward the vision for the school, but it is important for governors to be involved as much as possible so that everyone knows how they can help deliver aspirations for the whole community. One good way to contribute to the creation or re-setting of a vision statement is for the full governing body to ask itself three questions.

In three years time:

1. What do we want to be *saying* about the school?

2. How will we want to *feel* about the school?

3. What will we want to be *doing* as governors?

This can be done quickly in an activity in pairs or threes using felt-tip pens and sticky notes, putting them up on a flipchart. This will provide a whole host of ideas. Three governors could then take the flipchart away, group the ideas and produce a sentence or two for each question.

Action planning: how we are going to achieve the vision

A development plan is the usual way of staying on track. There are plenty of different formats but whichever one you choose, the following elements are essential.

- Action
- Intended outcome
- How will we know it has worked?
- Who will do it and who will check it is being done?
- When will the actions happen?
- With what resources (e.g. money, staff time, governors' time, space)?

Communication: how we are doing so far

Lots of schools grumble about poor communication. The solution is usually more emails, newsletters and staff bulletins – sending out an avalanche of information and solving the wrong problem. This often makes the problem worse because, with their portable devices and access to the internet wherever they are, staff (and governors) may feel obliged to check for incoming messages at all hours of the day and night.

For every action, the key lists to make are:

- Who do we need to consult before we act?

- Who do we need to inform about the action before we do it? How?
- Who do we need to inform that the action has taken place? How?

It may take time initially but it will save time in the long run.

Making minutes really useful

The chair (or clerk) should only record comments (anonymously) if absolutely necessary. The minute-taker should read out what they have recorded at the end of each agenda item and agree any corrections. This means you don't need to waste time at the start of the next meeting by agreeing that the minutes are accurate – you can get straight into finding out whether everyone has done what they said they would do.

Only allow any other business or an extension to the length of the meeting if the chair senses that those present are in agreement. Always give attendees the opportunity to leave at the agreed end time.

The clerk will always take full governing body minutes so that they comply with any legal or other guidance.

Meeting evaluation checklist

Standards in schools rise when they know what they are aiming to achieve, how they are currently doing and take effective action to address any weaknesses.

Appendix 4 comprises a checklist of characteristics to enable chairs to manage meetings effectively (what are we aiming to achieve?) and a space for a grade (how are we currently doing?). This principle of making our own accurate judgements, and not waiting for an external judgement from Ofsted or anyone else, is effective evaluation.

Evaluation is the key to continuous quality improvement. It is the main theme of the next chapter, where it will become clear how you might use this checklist.

Chapter 2

Good governance:
the importance of self-evaluation
and effective policies

This chapter will:

- Provide a practical toolkit for the governing body to improve itself
- Give clear advice about how to make sure policies are working as they should
- Help you become familiar with the vocabulary and processes school staff use in improving the quality of education for pupils

Self-evaluation: the dominant school improvement strategy

The Ofsted inspection schedule is a powerful mechanism which is used by the government to influence schools. One aspect of inspection focuses on the self-evaluation process in which schools assess their own performance against the same criteria used by Ofsted. The self-evaluation form (SEF) has become the dominant mechanism for raising standards in schools and, as a governor, it will be a key document for you to regularly scrutinise.

There are three key arguments for governing bodies to engage in self-evaluation:

1. If we want continuous improvement in our provision for pupils we have to model that practice: know where we are, design an intervention, implement it and measure the improvement.

2. There is no such thing as a perfect individual but we can create a perfect team. We need to know what our weaknesses are – our skills and knowledge gaps – and then fill them.

3. A governing body that knows itself well is providing effective leadership in this area.

An effective self-evaluation process will cover the following questions:

- What are we aiming to achieve overall?
- What measures are we using as the key indicators to judge ourselves against?
- What is our target for each measure?
- What are we doing to achieve the targets we have set?

■ To what extent is what we are doing actually working?

■ Are we on track to achieve our targets?

■ How do we know?

■ What do we need to do next?

Schools can choose their own SEF from the various formats available. Whatever form is used, however, this is such an important document that governing bodies should make sure it is a main agenda item at least once a term.

The SEF is a powerful contributor to an inspection team's understanding of the quality of leadership and management in a school. Governing bodies need to model this leadership behaviour with a full review annually as well as interim reviews when the head teacher is revising the leadership and management section of the SEF.

This exercise is not simply about the mechanical activity of filling in a form to record self-evaluation; it is that the *improvement in outcomes* constitutes evidence that self-evaluation is working and actually making a difference.

The governing body should carry out an annual audit of the skills, knowledge and experience that governors contribute to the governing body. The following questions work well:

■ What aspects of school life particularly interest you as a governor?

■ What would you like to do more of as a governor in the coming year?

- What would you like to do less of?
- What skills, knowledge and experience do you have that we can make good use of if the opportunity arises?

Full governing body: a self-evaluation checklist

The form in Appendix 5 uses the Ofsted grading criteria which can be used by chairs to evaluate the governing body. Items evaluated as grades 3 and 4 can be transferred to the leadership section of the school improvement plan. This provides clear evidence of good leadership by the governing body: using accurate self-evaluation to identify *and tackle* any weaknesses.

This should be completed by the full governing body under the leadership of the chair. It is best taken at a good pace with only a minimum of discussion. This will contribute to ensuring that self-evaluation is embedded firmly in the culture of the school (i.e. how we do things round here). It is also a good team-building activity.

Self-evaluation: two quick and effective methods

Method 1

At least annually, a governor could be invited to simply observe the meeting. They could feed back using the effective meetings framework in Appendix 4.

Method 2

Once a term, the chair could end the meeting by inviting feedback from everyone present. One person could record comments verbatim onto a flipchart. The chair should not respond immediately to any views, but simply say 'Thank you'. All feedback is valuable and therefore should not be challenged.

First ask: *What went well?* Invite comments and write them up. Once this has been completed invite comments on what could be improved: *It would have been even better if ...*

There are two common criticisms of SEFs:

1. In a poor quality SEF, there is too much space devoted to *what we are doing*: that is, descriptions of the school, its aims, its curriculum, its activities. These have their place – but that place is the school prospectus, website or Facebook page.

2. An outstanding SEF will comprise judgements about the quality of provision, about *how we are doing,* with brief references to the context. Essentially it should be bullet points evaluating provision with a column for recording where evidence to prove the judgement can be found.

Good governance: policies

Schools need to have policies in place for three reasons:

1. It may be a legal requirement

2. It may be a requirement of being one of a chain of schools[5]

3. A school may find it needs a policy unique to its context

Policies should drive practice and your job as governor is to work with the head teacher to make sure that they are not just a paper exercise but are actually used in school. They are critical to both leadership – getting us to where we want to get to – and management – getting there as quickly and efficiently as possible.

The list of policies that are currently required and recommended is readily available from the Department for Education.[6] It is too important to simply rely on the list on pages 41-42 (correct at the time of writing) because it will quickly be out of date. However, it is included to provide an indication of the sorts of policies required. A web search will also turn up model policies from other schools. So there really is no need for a school to start with a blank sheet – unless you need a policy on how to use circus skills in maths teaching!

Policies will need to be reviewed at different intervals; however, all policies must have a review interval allocated.

The four vital functions of policies are:

1. To lead practice, as decided by the school itself

Example: Homework. Data shows that homework does not consistently have the desired impact on learning. A staff working group is formed to review the school's homework policy and propose any changes necessary. After implementation of the changes, the working group evaluates the effectiveness of the revised policy.

2. To lead practice, as set from outside the school

    Example: Equality Act 2010. This Act covers all types of unlawful discrimination relating to sex, race, disability, religion/belief and sexual orientation. Schools cannot discriminate against pupils on any of these grounds and must publish equality information and objectives.

3. To ensure consistency in high-risk policy areas

    High-risk policies must be kept up to date because the requirements are often statutory. They are therefore subject to frequent changes in the law. Typically, this will include all personnel policies (also known as human resources or HR), health and safety and safeguarding policies. These are 'high risk' because inconsistencies will almost always cause conflicts that should have been avoided and which always take up time, emotional energy and money. More importantly, inconsistencies may cause harm to individuals or groups.

4. To ensure consistency of practice and help everyone get things right first time

    These are 'do this – it works' policies. They are the ones you are most likely to see on a desk or shelf as they are referred to frequently. Amongst these will be the school's policy on charging parents for activities, organising trips and residential visits, implementing home–school agreements and managing exclusions, complaints or admissions. Often the policy will contain templates for letters and other necessary documents.

Policy review

It must be obvious by now that policies are of no use whatsoever if they are not reliable. The purpose of a review is to ensure the school's policies are:

1. Up to date, especially legally

2. Easy to locate

3. Well written so that they are easy to understand and to use

In addition, a policy review will identify two important gaps:

1. The difference between the policy and what is actually happening in school

2. The difference between what the policy was intended to achieve and what it is actually achieving

These gaps have to be bridged. The process involves assigning a priority to this work, designing the bridge and then implementing it. This procedure can risk turning a policy review into a drawn-out task which deflects the leadership of the school, especially governors, from top priority activities. However, efficient and effective policy review is an essential part of leadership and of the day-to-day management of the school. The challenge, therefore, is how to allocate just enough time so that you achieve the benefits.

There are three main possibilities:

1. Contract with an external provider to undertake a policy review

   This will involve identifying a HR company, specialist law firm, local authority or school improvement services provider. At one end of the spectrum you can pay someone to plan and lead school-based activities, for example, consultations with governors, staff and staff associations. At the other end of the spectrum, the review can be funded as a desk activity by reading the relevant documents and comparing them with best practice examples. This leaves the school to identify and bridge the gaps identified above.

2. Set up a task-and-finish group

   This group can be created annually to work intensively for a short period. Who participates is a matter of tradition and culture: for example, it might be volunteers or chairs of committees. What matters is that the group achieves its remit.

3. Set up a standing group

This group will be on the annual meetings calendar and will meet as frequently as necessary to fulfil the remit. A standing group differs from a committee as it is established for a single purpose and only meets and reports back when needed.

Whichever option is chosen, the governing body will need to brief the relevant parties by agreeing a remit. There are common elements to a remit for any type of review group. The group will have responsibility for bringing to the attention of the full governing body an annual statement which will judge the extent to which, taken together, the school's policies currently reflect best practice, the school's needs and any statutory requirements.

Then, for *each policy* under review:

1. Identify if any gaps exist and, if so …

2. Propose how to bridge them, including any training needs and how they will be met.

3. Identify significant changes between previous and current versions of the policy and explain why the changes are needed and what they are intended to achieve.

4. List discussion points that the group advises the full governing body to consider before ratification.

This will make it possible for a full governors' meeting to focus discussion precisely where it is needed and ratify policies efficiently, referring back to the group only those issues that cannot be resolved in the time allocated.

There are usually more than 50 policies in a school. They can become a distraction rather than a driver of change and reliable help in the day-to-day management of the school – but only if we *let* them.

Statutory policies and other statutory documents

Not all of these policies apply to all schools – hence, this list is provided only to give an indication of the breadth and quantity needed. Your head teacher and the DfE website will have up-to-date information. This list will, however, help governors to ask the right questions about which ones should apply to your school.

1. Statutory policies required by education legislation:
   - Charging for activities
   - Appraisal
   - School behaviour
   - Sex education
   - Special educational needs
   - Teachers' pay

2. Statutory policies required by other legislation which impact particularly on schools:
   - Data protection
   - Health and safety

3. Other statutory documents:
   - Admissions arrangements
   - Accessibility plans
   - Central record of recruitment checks
   - Complaints procedure
   - Freedom of information
   - Governors' expenses and allowances
   - Governors' annual report to parents
   - Home–school agreement
   - Instruments of government
   - Minutes of meetings of the governing body and its committees, with copies of any documents used at the meetings
   - Premises
   - Publication of equality information and objectives
   - Register of business interests of governors
   - Register of pupils
   - Staff capability, discipline, conduct and grievance procedures

You may have noticed an obvious gap – safeguarding (also referred to as child protection). This is because there is no statutory requirement to have a policy, but there *is* statutory guidance which recommends that schools have a policy on safeguarding children and safer recruitment.

Any school would need a very good reason not to have policies covering these areas. I can't think of one. This is an example of where there is no need for a law to make us do the right and obvious thing.

Key points

1. You are responsible for having certain statutory policies as a governing body.

2. These need to be regularly reviewed – usually every two years or when the law changes.

3. The policy should drive practice in the school; that is what governors are responsible for, so make sure it does!

4. Don't get so bogged down with creating or updating policies that the role of governors in your school becomes a paper-shifting exercise.

5. Check that policies are being implemented when you visit the school and take part in meetings.

6. There are plenty of model policies available online to download.

7. Delegate detailed policy-writing and updating to relevant committees.

Chapter 3

Governor visits to the school

This chapter will provide:

■ Reasons why governor visits are essential
■ Full guidance to make sure that visits are a wholly positive experience for all concerned

How do governor visits contribute to good governance?

Being a governor is not just about attending meetings. It also involves evaluating the school's leadership team on the basis of what happens in the school on a daily basis and the only way to do this is to visit during the school day – once a term is about right. It used to be a requirement of local authorities that they should 'know their schools well'. Now that is a duty of the governing body.

This visit advice applies to schools of any phase. However, size makes a difference. For example, a smaller staff team in a primary or nursery school often gets together in one staff-room where you might be able to say hello to everyone. If there's a 'Today's Visitors' board you may be able to point to yourself on it.

In secondary schools, the staff are much more dispersed and a visit will almost certainly only take in a small section of the school. There may be eight or more science lessons all going on at once, so simply calling in on each of these will take up your entire visit time.

Outstanding leadership and management

The January 2012 Ofsted Evaluation Schedule for school inspection describes 'outstanding' leadership and management as follows:

> All leaders and managers, including the governing body, are highly ambitious for the school and lead by example. They base their actions on a deep and accurate understanding of the school's performance and of staff and pupils' skills and attributes. Key leaders focus relentlessly on improving teaching and learning, resulting in teaching that is likely to be outstanding and at least consistently good.[7]

The guidance on leadership and management also adds that inspectors will focus on 'how relentlessly leaders, managers and the governing body pursue a vision for excellence' (p. 18) and then goes on to illustrate how they can do it. They will also look for evidence of 'effective work by the governing body that acts as a critical friend and holds senior leaders to account for all aspects of the school's performance' (p. 19).

Why do school visits?

How can school governors get to know the school sufficiently to be able to challenge senior leaders – especially when governors rely heavily on the head teacher and senior staff for information at their meetings?

It is possible to get some insights into how the school performs from informal contact with parents, particularly if you live in the local community. You may acquire information from your own children in the school or from those of family, neighbours and friends. These can all be useful sources but, equally, can be dangerously anecdotal. Any stories you hear will need to be checked for accuracy but at least this can give a general idea of how well (or badly) the school is thought of locally. Don't keep these stories to yourself. Let the head teacher or other senior leaders know what you are hearing. Another resource is Parent View on the Ofsted website. Governing body meetings should also assist in giving you a real feel for how the school runs.

But there is no substitute for actually visiting the school. Formal (because they are recorded), focused, daytime visits provide the information and evidence which enable governors to act as informed critical friends to the school leadership. Try also to make some informal visits, such as attending school events and functions or 'dropping in' to lessons when invited. Dropping in means exactly that – a relaxed opportunity to see what is going on. Visits are an enjoyable and an essential part of being a governor and will really help you get to know the school, its staff and pupils, and how well it all works. Of course, you are not an inspector of any kind and it is always worth reminding ourselves that governors and staff are all on the same side.

Why visit during the school day?

There are four main reasons to visit during daytime hours:

1. To see the school at work. Most governing bodies meet in the evenings – but an empty, quiet building is not the school.

2. To develop a 'one-team' approach with the staff, who enjoy a chance to show off their work and that of their pupils. They will think more of a governing body if they know that governors make the time to come in and see the school in action.

3. To carry out focused reviews on aspects of school life on behalf of the governing body (e.g. an issue raised in a

previous Ofsted report or a current issue regarding implementation or monitoring of a school policy).

4. Because the governing body will be better informed about the day-to-day routines and better able to take account of the school context – and the staff will know this too.

Daytime visits are best but there may also be evenings when pupils will be at the school, so you can still make visits to fit around your daytime commitments. The cleaning team and caretaking or facilities staff will also welcome the opportunity to discuss their work, even if they are not direct employees of the school.

Early years settings of every sort, as well as primary schools, are used to visitors and volunteers. This makes it easy to slip in and be one of the crowd. Sit on the floor in a nursery area and you'll find within a few minutes that children are bringing things over to show you and ask you about.

One final piece of persuasive argument for making visits rather than just relying on second-hand information comes from Barry Primary School, Northampton. These three points of praise for governors and one of criticism come from the school's September 2012 Ofsted inspection report:

Governors fulfil their statutory duties and review the school's performance regularly. They contribute to strategic planning and have supported changes in procedure such as the behaviour policy.

However, they rely mostly on information supplied by senior staff rather than gathering evidence themselves.

Making the time for a visit

You may be in full-time work and have the sort of job where someone has to take over if you are away, or you may work somewhere where time off other than for illness and holidays is not usually permitted. School governors, except in academies, are entitled to reasonable time off work to perform this public service, and some organisations have a deep memory of this tradition so you may find it easier than you think to get permission.

Your manager should already know that you are a school governor. If they don't, tell them now. Then, after a decent interval, ask if it is possible to come in late one morning or leave early so that you can make a governor visit. Depending on your workplace, you could offer to take time as unpaid leave of absence, make up the hours or use holiday leave. However, all employers should support you to take time off to visit a school as part of their contribution to the community, including as an academy governor.

If you are in a senior position yourself, first let your colleagues know that you are a governor and that you will look favourably on school visit requests from them if they are governors. Then plan your own visit.

If you are in charge of your own diary – lucky you! Take your pick of interesting days to visit.

Chapter 3

How to set up a visit

If governor visits are not part of the typical work of your governing body, tell the chair that you would like to come back to them with some thoughts on the benefits of governor visits. Read this chapter and start raising the idea of visits with staff and governors. In other words, start planting the seeds and watering them.

Where governor visits are established, ask for a brief meeting at the school with the head teacher or a member of the senior leadership team. Reference to 'head teacher' below includes any member of staff to whom they delegate the task of hosting your visit. 'Classroom' means any learning space – and that might include playing fields, so wear suitable footwear!

You might ask the head teacher:

- What they think about governor visits so far
- What has gone well in the past – and what has not
- Suggestions for a focus
- Whether it is appropriate for a pupil to show you around

Let the head teacher know if you are especially interested in a particular area of school life. Be clear about what you want to learn and what questions you need to ask in order to cover this. Many governors become the 'link governor' to certain departments or areas of the school, such as special needs.

Finally, ask who you should speak to if you see behaviour towards any pupil or member of staff that needs to be reported. Safeguarding young people's well-being is something we are all responsible for, all the time. Being attentive to the welfare of staff is also a part of the governors' role.

Top tips for creating the perfect visit ☑

In your talk with the head teacher you should:

1. Agree a focus for the visit. Be clear about what you are working towards before you begin. It might be to see how a particular priority in the school improvement plan is being addressed in practice or as part of routine review of how a particular policy is working.

2. Agree a date. Visits can take time to arrange as the staff you may want to see must be consulted. Then it has to match with your own diary, staff timetables and the school diary.

3. Find out about the etiquette of school visits. Supplement this by phoning or emailing other governors who have visited already; there may be a particular form to fill in, for example. Certainly there will be agreed factors that make for successful governor visits in your school. Ask how to find out

what you may want to know about without upsetting the staff, especially when giving feedback.

4. Agree a visit schedule. Once the head teacher has settled on a date and consulted staff, they will send you a visit schedule based on which staff and pupils are available and what is going on that day. Schools run on timetables – so you should get one too! For a visit of about two hours it may follow a pattern similar to this:

▨ A few minutes with the head teacher who will make any final adjustments to the schedule.

▨ The visit – about an hour. If you are going to see more than one classroom this will be tightly scheduled and there will be someone – probably a pupil – who will accompany you to your next class. Make it clear whether you would prefer to be accompanied by a member of staff, especially on your first visit. Having this support may help you to avoid any possible difficulties and give you some welcome feedback.

▨ Refreshments in the staffroom – ten minutes to take the opportunity to introduce yourself to anyone in the room and explain who you are and why you are enjoying your visit so much.

■ A few minutes to collect your thoughts and make some notes. Check back to the purpose of the visit and stick to it.

■ Fifteen minutes for feedback with the head teacher.

5. Decide how you want to record your observations. Ask if you can take written notes in any meetings with staff or pupils. It is unlikely you will be refused but it is sensible to check. For example, it may be agreed that all notes will be left in a file at the school.

Making notes during a meeting actually helps with more than just supporting your memory – it shows that you think that what people are telling you is important. Making notes on a laptop or tablet can be intrusive and distracting, although this may change as tablets become more common.

If there is an approved governors' lesson observation form (there is an example in Appendix 6), ask for training in its use and do at least one paired visit. Be very attentive to advice about how to word comments. Teachers are – rightly – sensitive about judgements made by those who are not qualified teachers. This is why there may be a separate lesson visit form for governors to use. Follow precisely all school policies on the use of cameras and sound recording equipment.

6. Ask the head if there is anything you need to keep confidential.

7. Agree whom you will report back to and how.

Five pieces of advice

1. Pupils – especially teenagers – can sometimes show off in front of visitors. They may misbehave or cause low-level disruption. If you feel this is happening, simply thank the teacher for allowing you to visit and leave. Make sure you feed back to the teacher why you left and that you do not have any concerns about what you observed – the teacher was simply doing their job. Perhaps ask them how they feel about it. They may worry that poor behaviour by pupils will reflect badly on them and that you will make judgements about their ability to manage pupil behaviour.

2. When moving around the school you may come across a member of staff dealing with poor student behaviour. Make yourself invisible.

3. You should be extremely cautious about identifying pupils, students and staff in reports or in any other indiscrete way. This is another area where you should follow school policies and practice with precision.

4. If you expect to be able to visit regularly, why not ask for more specific training? Perhaps a member of staff can train you in observation skills – how to interpret what you are seeing and how to use appropriate parts of the agreed lesson observation record. This will make your time even more useful to the pupils and staff. But, remember, you are still not an inspector!

5. Finally, an older student who is showing you around will certainly appreciate it if you explain that you would like to sit down with them at some point during the tour and have a more detailed conversation.

Breaks and lunchtimes

Your schedule should include a member of staff being with you at breaktimes. If they are on duty, go with them. Seeing the pupils and staff together in what is referred to as 'unstructured time' is another opportunity to get a real understanding of how the school works.

School lunches are served in most schools, so join in. If it's packed lunches only, remember to take yours with you.

Tim Read, chair of governors at Elizabeth Woodville School, Northamptonshire has the following advice on governor visits to classrooms:

- Visiting in pairs is helpful.

- Sit alongside two pupils and ask them: How are you getting on? What level are you working at? How do you know? What are your most recent marks?

- Teenage pupils are reticent with adults. If necessary, ask staff for clarification.

Learning walks

'Learning walk' may sound a bit like jargon. What it means is a planned walk through as much of the school as possible, with particular aims in mind and using a learning walk record form to fill in any observations. If you would rather not do a learning walk on your first visit, just say so. If you do one with a teacher then clearly they will be in a position to make formal judgements about the quality of teaching and learning. These will be evidence for the school's self-evaluation process.

In a secondary school, for example, you might visit the end of a lesson to see how the recent training on plenaries has been implemented or walk the corridors before the next lesson to observe whether pupils' punctuality to lessons has improved. In a primary school, it might mean visiting every classroom to judge the extent to which pupils are using displays to aid their learning. In a nursery school, you may be evaluating the role of learning support assistants in recording pupils' use of spoken language.

Talk through learning walks with the head teacher and ask to see any examples of previous checklists or record sheets. If not, here are some useful starting points.

Giving helpful and welcome feedback to staff

Giving feedback at the end of a visit is important – whether it is a learning walk, classroom visit, an informal meeting with staff and pupils or attendance at a school council meeting.

> I made the mistake of saying to the head at the end of the day that I thought the primary classrooms I had visited were cluttered. 'I think you mean visually stimulating with lots of the children's work on display?' the head suggested, gently.
>
> > Inexperienced primary school governor –
> > suitably chastened (I admit it!
> > This was me – and it *was* a long time ago)

It will help if you reflect on what it is like when you are formally observed at work. If no one has ever observed you, then try to imagine what it must feel like to be observed. Consider also how teaching staff may feel about being observed by someone who is not an expert teacher. This is why it is best for your comments to be solely about the focus of the visit (e.g. how well the new tablet computers are being used, how many pupils know what level they are working at). You are not a trained inspector so avoid commenting on matters like the quality of teaching, progress made by pupils during the lesson or the accuracy of assessment. Always directly relate any comments to what you have seen.

Staff in schools have respect for governors and know them to be an important element in the leadership and management of the school. Anything you do and say will be remembered and shared.

The two golden rules of great feedback are:

1. Start with all the good things. Use the nine-to-one ratio – make nine compliments for one concern. Despite this, you can be fairly certain that only the worry will be followed up in conversation with you.

2. Praise in public, blame in private. Your concern may be unfounded and if you voice it in front of others you won't be able to control the response. In private, you can frame a concern as a question, for example:

   ▓ Is it usual to ...?

   ▓ Am I right in thinking that when I saw ...?

- One of your colleagues said ... is that a common view?

- I saw three Year 11 students being extremely loud, rude and disrespectful to a member of staff in a classroom. I moved away at once. What happens in these situations?

- Could you tell me a little more about ...

Top tips for the day of the visit ☑

- Don't carry a clipboard.
- Dress the way staff dress.
- Have the focus for the visit written in a pad or notebook where you can refer to it easily.
- Take relevant notes.
- Look friendly.
- Don't show your feelings if you think things are going wrong.
- Smile, especially with your eyes!
- If a pupil is rude to you say something, quietly, like: 'I'll come back in a few minutes when you can speak with me with more respect' or 'I disapprove of how you are speaking to me, and will therefore speak with someone else' or 'As a school governor I know that it is important to listen and to speak with respect. Shall we start again?'

▨ You may be invited to participate. (Perhaps you know enough to help in a GCSE French lesson?) Whether you are happy to be asked, or would prefer not to be, make that part of your visit preparation so staff know in advance.

▨ Every teacher welcomes brief feedback – try to see them before you leave and say in what ways you enjoyed being in their lesson.

▨ Sometimes visitors to a classroom forget to greet a teaching assistant as well as the teacher, often because they are sitting in amongst the pupils. At least try to catch their eye and smile.

▨ The teacher will usually suggest what you do, where you sit and who you talk to, so they will really appreciate you reminding them of the focus of your visit and how long you can be with them.

▨ Staff are generally very used to having other adults in the classroom with them. However, they deliberately create a sense that this is *their* classroom – a place where *they* are in charge – because it is part of good behaviour management. Imagine you are entering someone's front room that just happens to be full of 8-year-olds or 15-year-olds. Providing you haven't walked into a silent task, feel free to greet the class: 'Good morning, everyone.' If it is an appropriate moment, or you are invited to do so, say who you are and explain that you are a school governor – an expert volunteer who helps the leadership team.

▪ If appropriate, talk to the pupils because you will learn so much from them. Ask questions about their lesson and what they have achieved and enjoy at school.

▪ Keep in mind at all times the head teacher's guidance on confidentiality.

Reporting back to governors

If reporting back is new for you, you might start by reporting back to the relevant committee first rather than to the whole governing body. Filling in the final version of the governor visit form or learning walk form in preparation for reporting back should now be straightforward: when you gave feedback to the head teacher and staff you had the chance to test your observations and can now adjust your comments.

Although you are not an inspector, it will help to use words and phrases that are clear and show judgement, for example:

The students in Year 11 were very well behaved and most were obviously really enjoying learning science. Those who weren't so keen did get on with the work but with fewer questions to the staff.

Lunchtime was really interesting for the children in Key Stage 1 – on Mondays they have a play assistant which is why I chose play as my focus (Mondays are my only free day). The children show high levels of respect for each other. They took turns and helped each other, with very little prompting from either of us adults. They especially looked out for the two shy children and the child with special needs.

If you are reporting back to the full governing body make sure that you stick closely to the time you are allocated – finish early if possible. This will mean everyone pays full attention and doesn't start peering at their agenda or glancing at the chair! If you have more to say, you can always give a written report to the clerk to be circulated afterwards with the minutes. Hand the document over (or say you will email it) at the start of your remarks so that the clerk knows they do not need to take notes and can concentrate on what you have to say and on any questions or comments.

Try to follow these guidelines:

1. Recap the focus of the visit – what did you want to learn?

2. What you did – a brief description based on the visit schedule.

3. What you learnt – any examples to share: pupils' work you have borrowed, a direct quote from a student or member of staff, etc.

4. How you feel about what you learnt.

5. Invite questions or comments.

Recap: why governors love to visit their schools

- It is rewarding in itself.

- It is one of the real privileges of serving as a governor to be in the school, with the right to ask questions and to go anywhere the staff and pupils can go.

- In any area of life, there is nothing more moving and memorable than seeing children and young people contentedly doing things together, and with adults who care about them. Your school will be a great place to see this in action.

- Knowing the school well becomes much more rewarding than simply knowing the data sets.

Chapter 4

Holding the head teacher and leadership team to account

> This chapter will:
>
> ▪ Define accountability in the context of the governing body's strategic leadership role
>
> ▪ Provide a sequence of questions and tips on how to carry out this function

What we really mean

Holding to account is another term we come across regularly as governors. It is one of the main functions of the governing body. If strategic leadership is setting the direction and ensuring we are on the right path, holding to account is its twin: asking the right questions of the right people to ensure they are doing what they are supposed to be doing to get us there.

The terms *challenge* and *support* are used frequently in relation to holding someone to account. Challenge means to probe further by asking questions. It does not mean being aggressive or taking the stance of a forceful radio or TV interviewer. Broadcasters often give the interviewee and the audience the impression that they don't really believe the interviewee is telling the whole truth. Governors, staff and parents are all on the same side; we ask each other questions in order to test our thinking and our practice.

The most important thing governors should know about is the progress pupils are making in the school. Given their individual starting points: Where are they now? Are they doing as well as they should? As well as they could? The responses to these enquiries give us the answer to the following question: What difference are *we* making?

The key elements of effective accountability processes

Outcomes: What you need to know about data

Schools generate a lot of data. A typical primary school with 200 pupils on RAISEonline produced 97 pages of data in autumn 2012. This can be overwhelming for school leadership teams, so here are two pieces of advice:

1. Governors must insist that the head teacher (and their staff) turn data into *information*. A graph can be very helpful but it is the information derived from it that

matters. For example, the data from a graph might be turned into the statement: *The graph shows that pupils in middle-ability groups are making better progress in English than in mathematics.*

2. Governors must decide, along with the head teacher, what the key data sets are and what information the governing body wants to receive based on that data. In addition, head teachers must be free to choose other data from all the statistics available to illustrate a particular issue.

It is not necessary for governors to know their scattergrams from their Venn diagrams. However, it is essential for governors to be sure what key information they currently want and to ask for it in a form that enables them to ask the right questions. For example: Why, exactly, are middle-ability groups making better progress in English than mathematics? What are we as a school doing to close the gap?

Tip ☑

Keep the right focus by asking: What is this data and information telling us?

Head teacher's report

The agenda of every full governing body meeting should include a head teacher's report. The head teacher's report is the centrepiece of the meeting because it contains information provided by the school's most senior professional. It will have taken a large number of staff hours to put together – collating data and turning it into information is a skilled and time-consuming business. The report is the governors' window into the school: it frames how they see it and helps them to identify emerging issues and priorities.

The report needs adequate time devoted to it to ensure that its valuable content has been fully explored. The outcomes of the agenda item will dictate the approach. There may be items in the report that the head teacher wishes the governing body to note, provide a view on or take a decision about. The chair will need to identify these points and allocate time to them, preferably in the final section of the head teacher's report agenda item, so that these matters do not take time from the core agenda item – holding the head teacher to account.

How the report is presented is critical. It should have been circulated in advance, but even so, there may be governors present who have not had time to read it, there may be new governors in attendance or there may be staff observers present for the first time.

Head teacher's report: a suggested approach

Taking into consideration all the points set out above, it makes sense for governors to have an opportunity to engage with the report itself. Chairs of meetings are often reluctant to let go and move away from the model of one person talking at a time and the chair choosing who that will be. However, this is an opportunity when the chair could either allow a period for silent reading or suggest those present pair up to read and discuss the report together. Longer will be needed for this option, but it can be more suitable if there are new governors or observers present. The task set in each case will be to identify possible questions.

The item can then proceed by the chair inviting the head teacher to introduce their report; for example, by amplifying the following first two questions in the report itself:

Overall, what has been the quality of provision, by key stage, over the first half term?

What are the current self-evaluation judgements for the five key Ofsted measures?

1. Overall effectiveness

2. Achievement of pupils at the school

3. Quality of teaching in the school

4. Behaviour and safety of pupils at the school

5. Quality of leadership in, and management of, the school (including governance)

Then the head can take questions. This is where the chair takes control again in the usual way of choosing the order and guiding the meeting through to completion of this item.

Head teacher's report: some suggested headings

Whilst it is a matter for the governing body to decide the format for reports delivered to them, if changes are proposed to current practice then they must be well managed. The head teacher is likely to have well-founded views, and it is their report after all.

In Appendix 8 is a list from which you may wish to select certain elements. As a discussion starter, the chair could ask: Which of these headings and questions might we want to use?

Good practice in effective questions will soon spread from the full governing body meeting into all other committees and meetings; it will embed itself into your way of working well together.

A governing body that takes this supportive approach in its meetings is holding the head teacher and senior leaders properly to account.

Ideas for discussion

▪ When there are five full governing body meetings in a year, three might focus on head teacher reports, one could consider the self-evaluation form and the other the school improvement plan.

▪ If there is a sixth meeting it might be the opportunity for another member of the leadership team to present a report on behalf of the whole team – a fresh set of eyes can be illuminating both in terms of content and approach. Give them creative freedom to tell the story about what a great year it has been so far in whatever way they decide will work best.

Effective appraisal of the head teacher

There are two aspects to appraisal (also known as performance management): the head teacher's review and the effectiveness of the school's overall appraisal system. Governors appraise the head teacher and, as part of the process, must engage an external adviser; whom they choose is entirely a matter for the governing body.

New regulations for teachers were introduced in 2012. They give schools a great deal of freedom in relation to appraisal and the DfE guidance is incorporated into a model appraisal policy.[8] This is in line with the government's strategy of increasing school autonomy and reducing the volume of guidance

Assuming the school has adopted the model policy (with any adjustments to suit the local situation), the only other requirement is for the head teacher to know what standards they are being appraised against. The model policy only mentions the Teacher Standards (revised and re-issued in 2012)[9] but there are also National Standards for Headteachers (published in 2004).[10] A selection of expectations from these standards can be tailored to fit the context of the school.

It would hardly be in keeping with the slimmed down guidance to amplify it here with a lot of advice, but I cannot resist just two key tips!

Tips ☑

- Focus on objectives that the head teacher, and *only* the head teacher, can achieve. This keeps the attention on mid- and longer-term objectives: over perhaps two or three years. There will be agreed annual milestones towards achieving them. In addition, there may be urgent areas that need an annual completion date. Including the success criteria for objectives will make it easier to decide how much progress has been made a year later.

- The head teacher will need to produce enough evidence to demonstrate the extent to which they have achieved an objective or any targets along the way. Discussing together and listing this evidence can be a powerful way of directing the appraisal process and making it truly effective.

Appraisal of the whole staff (and Ofsted)

Staff costs usually amount to around 80% of the entire school budget. It is appropriate for governors to hold staff to account for this expenditure, both by focusing on educational outcomes for pupils and on the quality of the staff's work as key public sector employees. Accordingly, it is good practice for all staff members to have an annual appraisal, not just teachers.

The annual head teacher's report should contain an evaluation of the effectiveness of the entire appraisal process in achieving the school's strategic aims. It should record the extent to which staff objectives are aligned with school improvement priorities and the degree to which objectives are tailored to individual needs.

Over the last ten years there has been an increased emphasis on linking performance with pay. Whilst this must be sensitively managed, it is a clear direction of travel nationally. Asking the head teacher for anonymised data on the extent to which appraisal informs pay decisions will begin to give governors an insight into this subject. Pay is one of the policy areas that must be up to date and any changes should be carefully managed, taking account of the practice of the school in consulting with staff. Governors who have been responsible for annual appraisal of the head teacher's performance will already have experience of the linking of appraisal and pay: a pay recommendation is part of the head teacher appraisal process.

The effectiveness of appraisal is one of Ofsted's indicators for making a judgement about leadership and management. Inspectors are asked to consider:

- *the robustness of performance management and effectiveness of strategies for improving teaching, including the extent to which the school takes account of the 'Teachers' Standards' – this is demonstrated through:*

- *the robustness of procedures for monitoring the quality of teaching and learning and the extent to which underperformance is tackled*
- *a strong link between performance management and appraisal and salary progression.*[11]

Handling complaints and parental concerns vs. managing compliments and positive suggestions

Complaints and compliments are two sides of the governors' role as a link between the school and the community it serves. Both provide additional evidence that the governing body can use to hold staff to account. When we keep our eyes and ears peeled we usually hear complaints – and may need to be even more alert to harvest compliments!

Complaints

External complaints should always be dealt with in line with the school's complaints policy. It can happen that a governor uses a full meeting to raise a grievance or concern of their own unannounced. It is best to prevent this turn of events by agreeing, as part of the annual review of the governing body's operating procedures, that this is unacceptable practice.

Governors' complaints, concerns and personal hobby horses all belong outside the meeting of the full governing body. A conversation with the chair of governors, during a governors' committee or in the head teacher's office are all better places for them to be raised.

Compliments

Governors and governing bodies should always pass on any praise they have come across and, indeed, should seek it out (from the Parent View area of the Ofsted website, and by routinely asking parents, 'What's going well here at the moment?'). Very often, all we hear are grumbles. The national media run too few good news stories, although the local press are much better in this respect. Compliments are particularly to be emphasised after a period when negative aspects of the school have come to the fore.

Good ideas are good ideas wherever they come from. This should be a core belief of all governors: it is part of the self-evaluation mindset that welcomes clear evaluation and the submission of solutions and suggestions. Always share good ideas. However, do think about when and who to share them with because there can be unexpected outcomes. You may enthusiastically share a great idea with the full governing body only to discover it was tried out two years ago and ended disastrously …

The special place of staff and parent governors

Staff and parent governors occupy a 'special place' because, when elections have been held, these two constituent groups feel a greater sense that the governor they elected should actually represent their views. One purpose of these governor roles is to promote good communication between the staff body, the parent body and the governing body. To achieve this, staff and parent governors often have to behave as if they are required to represent parent and staff views. This can cause misunderstandings. Staff and parents cannot ignore normal procedures and demand that a staff or parent governor argue a particular point of view, vote a particular way or raise a complaint in a full governing body meeting. All governors are equal; once appointed they have exactly the same responsibilities and duties.

To take advantage of the benefits of the 'special place', and at the risk of reinforcing uncertainty about the role of staff and parent governors, it remains good practice for staff and parent governors to make the agenda for the next meeting available to their constituent groups in an appropriate way. For staff, the best way may be online or on a noticeboard.

There are positives and negatives to each approach, as outlined below.

	Benefits	Concerns
Online	Staff can access the information at any time and anywhere to suit them. Increasingly widely used – lots of us post comments on forums so this is a good way to encourage engagement. Enables equal access to all.	Staff can access the information at any time and anywhere, so there is no escape! And they are usually alone when they read it, so cannot discuss it with colleagues. May produce an unmanageable volume of comments.
Noticeboard	Encourages discussion. Lends itself to dramatic presentation to attract attention to interesting items.	May not be seen by everyone, especially those working part-time. Takes time to manage, especially in large schools with several staff areas. A noticeboard where notices are more than two weeks out of date is not working as a means of communication.

Head teachers will know the preferred communication method for their own staff, including part-timers and regular volunteers, so seek their advice. Similarly, parent governors should find ways to make the agenda available to other parents, perhaps online, at the school gate, at a parents' evening or through the school website.

Pamela Hutchison, head teacher at Elizabeth Woodville School, Northamptonshire makes the following comments on parent and staff governors:

It is hard. As a parent, you can sign up to confidentiality, *but* you are still a parent of a child who will be affected by the decision. Similarly, the head teacher may be saying something that affects a staff governor personally – for example, reporting on the quality of teaching in a particular department. There is a subtle difference in what we expect of governors who are parents and parent governors.

Chapter 5

Ofsted: inspections and governors

This chapter aims to:

- Assist governors to play their part fully in ensuring a successful Ofsted inspection of their school
- Show how Ofsted fits into the long-term national strategy for improving schools
- Place Ofsted in its full context, showing how inspection has been an integral part of how schools have been run since the beginning of the state system
- Describe why Ofsted creates anxiety and stress and suggests how governors can play a part in reducing both

It is not a coincidence that the words *government*, *governance* and *governor* are almost identical. Governance refers to all the arrangements that surround the leadership and management of the school. However, since the 1960s, schools have increasingly been a matter for national attention, so this chapter begins with a basic outline of the roles of government, the state and parliament in education. It's a straightforward guide, so if you are already clear about these, skip straight to the section on local government.

Education is one of the services which has been devolved to Wales, Scotland and Northern Ireland, so the schooling systems of the four countries of the United Kingdom have been diverging since the start of this century.

National government

The national government at any one time will have policy objectives that differ from those of the opposition parties. The concept of the 'state' floats rather loftily above this and survives changes of government. Thus the state education system has a history and existence which is separate from government. Ofsted inspects both publicly funded and private providers of schools and other services to children and young people.

The term 'state education' is usually used to describe schools where there is no charge to attend them, but the *state's* education system includes all schools as well as children educated at home. There is no official figure for how many UK children are home-schooled, but it was estimated to be around 50,000 in 2010.[12] The state makes schooling compulsory for all children by requiring parents to educate them. It is for parents to decide how exactly to fulfil this legal duty, which includes home schooling.

Parliamentary committees often interview providers of services on our behalf or commission reports. Her Majesty's Chief Inspector of Schools has provided a report to parliament for over 100 years.

From 2015 the state will guarantee to provide a place of full-time education or training to age 18 – the raising of the participation age (RPA). At the moment, there are no plans to use the law to enforce attendance beyond the current school leaving age of 16.

Any government can change *how* the state delivers the services it provides. It might be through state ownership, services provided by private companies, local authorities or not-for-profit organisations such as trusts, charities, cooperatives and social enterprises. In the 21st century all these ways of running schools exist in the United Kingdom.

The governance of an individual school is provided by the governing body and almost always in partnership with others: the local authority, an academy trust or a formal link with one or more local schools. They provide long-term continuity. The local authority has a duty to monitor schools' performance and to plan ahead so that there are enough school places available in their area.

Local government

The provision of school places remains a duty for each local authority and is a very complex process. The authority needs to make sure there is a place for every child whose parents want one, including those with special educational needs.

The complexity arises because autonomy for schools can conflict with the state's responsibility to educate every child. If all schools had complete freedom to be whatever size they wanted or to open, close, move site or choose which pupils to educate, it would be impossible to guarantee a school place for every child. In addition, special schools are required for pupils with limited mobility, vision, hearing and so on, but the numbers in any one area may vary year on year and over time.

Our history has also provided us with faith schools, single-sex schools, schools with different pupil age ranges, fee-charging schools, schools that are run for profit, charitable schools and schools that only offer places to children of higher intellectual ability or with a talent for, say, dance. This means that this country's state education system is, most likely, one of the most diverse in the world. However, the range of schools available will be limited in any one area: only our very largest cities may contain one of each type of school.

Education reform

The creation of the Office for Standards in Education, Children's Services and Skills (Ofsted) was part of the strategy to bring education more under national government direction and raise standards through increasing schools' accountability.[13]

Standardised tables of examination results were published, which led to closer regulation of examinations. This meant comparisons could be made between schools (and other providers such as further education colleges). Regulation was needed because standards have to remain as constant as possible in order to make valid comparisons of year-on-year results between schools and different examination providers.

Regulation also stops any one provider of examinations cornering the market and making excessive profits by making their exams easy to pass. Freedom for schools to choose which qualifications to offer can only be provided by giving awarding bodies much *less* freedom in the content they test and how they test it.

Ofsted was established in order to raise standards through valid performance comparisons between schools and to track changes over time by inspecting all schools on a regular basis. Ofsted absorbed the work of Her Majesty's Inspectors of Schools (HMI). HMI still report formally to parliament on education matters, as they always have, and they are – as their name indicates – appointed to be *independent* of parliament. Ofsted inspections replaced local education authority inspections of schools in their area. These had been neither published nor reported to parliament. This activity to increase the accountability of schools was backed up by more regular inspections to a common standard and with reports published in a standard format.

Education as a 'market': using pressure from parents to raise standards

In order to increase competition between schools, local authorities lost the power to create school catchment areas. Formerly, pupils who lived in the catchment area of a particular school had to attend that school, although there was some flexibility for special cases.

Instead, parents now have the right to express a preference for the school they want their child to attend. This is often called 'parental choice'. A completely free market is not possible because the number of pupils a school can accept is determined by the size of the buildings (although some schools have been allowed to expand). Where there is more demand for places than are available, the school is classed as 'oversubscribed' – a description that is often used as a positive attribute. In the days of catchment areas, the only comparable indicator was that house prices were sometimes higher in the vicinity of popular schools.[14]

In sparsely populated rural areas there may be only one school within reasonable travelling distance – effectively limiting parental preference to a Hobson's choice.

Ofsted and schools: how do we respond to an Ofsted inspection?

Schools might naturally and properly be a touch apprehensive at the approach of an Ofsted inspection – rather as we might when buckling our seat belt next to the examiner at the start of a driving test. The truth is that Ofsted has not endeared itself to school staff and governors over the past 20 years, most of whom are much *more* than apprehensive, as MPs have observed:

> However, an element of healthy stress is a far cry from the 'headteachers and governors hamstrung by fear' which the Association of Teachers and Lecturers drew our attention to with regard to Ofsted inspection ... Social workers appear to agree that Ofsted has 'built a culture of negativity around inspection'.[15]

Ofsted does not refer to passing and failing *inspections*, but it does refer to failing *schools*. It is we who use pass and fail in relation to inspections, so those are the terms used in this chapter.

The significance of the outcomes of an Ofsted inspection are so great that the word Ofsted has acquired layers of meaning. It is of course an acronym but this can make the usage even more bewildering to someone not in the know:

- When was your last Ofsted?
- We'll be Ofstedded again in a year's time.
- What will Ofsted think about our new curriculum?
- Ofsted says we're outstanding.

Whatever the rights and wrongs of the matter, the fact is that anxiety is the dominant feeling which an Ofsted inspection inspires. Governors can help mitigate the effects of negative stress by being well prepared themselves and by routinely challenging and supporting staff – so that they know they can be confident of the outcome when an inspector calls.

If you fail your inspection: turning negatives into positives

A school with an overall grade of 4 will either be judged to have 'serious weaknesses' or to require 'special measures'. Schools with either of these judgements are often referred to as being 'in an Ofsted category'.

Staff and governors can feel that inspectors, focused as they are on outcomes for children and young people, simply don't take sufficient account of the context of the school. This is especially so when exam results are below local and national expectations and averages and when staff feel that this is because of circumstances outside their immediate control. For example, schools serving a community where parents have lower than average educational outcomes themselves, where there are few jobs for school leavers or where parents work long hours and can't give as much time as others to supporting their children's learning.

There are always schools in similar contexts whose outcomes are better and a great deal is done to share effective practice, including by Ofsted. But to staff and governors in a 'failing' school, it can feel as if the failure is their fault.

The consequences of failing an inspection are serious. It may be because the staff – and governors – are not performing well and deserve the grave consequences. Ofsted is simply doing what the pupils and parents need them to do to raise standards quickly and turn the school around. The entirely sound justification for this is that a 'failing school' is providing a poor quality education for the pupils – and it is their *only* chance to receive good quality schooling.

There are two issues for governors, in particular, to address if their school fails an inspection:

1. Staff and governors often feel that they are already doing their very best so can resist even well-founded criticism. Find someone to help you get through this response – to accept that 'we are where we are' not where we thought we were or hoped we were.

2. The impact on a school of failing an inspection can make things worse before they get better: governors need to act quickly to make this period as short as possible.

> We were put in special measures. We were already struggling. We felt like a drowning swimmer, and Ofsted threw us a lifebelt made of concrete.
>
> Secondary head teacher

When a school fails an inspection the head almost always resigns, so there may be a head teacher appointment for governors to make. Staff morale will be low, the local community will want to know that rapid improvements are on the way and pupils will wonder if they can still be proud of their school. Governors need to take a lead in all these areas.

Some governors may also step down. However, this will be an opportunity to appoint new recruits with specific skill sets who will be ready to take on the challenge of helping the school out of its current situation.

Ten top tips for governors to help their school ☑

1. Ask the right questions of the head about the school's performance – and make sure the head teacher's report and the minutes of every governors' meeting show clearly that this is happening.

2. Make certain that any issues identified in previous Ofsted inspection reports have been addressed and that the evidence is readily available.

3. Ensure that the school's self-evaluation document reads like an Ofsted inspection report and that issues are identified in priority order.

4. If the self-evaluation form indicates that there are areas where Ofsted will judge the school as requiring improvement, make those the top priorities for attention – immediately!

5. Insist that the school improvement plan includes all the identified issues with clear dates to start work on the lower priority issues and up-to-date information on where you are with the higher priority issues.

6. Understand how staff feel about inspections and keep in mind the purpose of this chapter: to show how Ofsted inspections fit in with the overall long-term national strategy of continuously improving the quality of education. Governors are part of government: this is their strategic role.

7. If there is any risk at all of failing your inspection, pay attention to the fact that inspectors have some discretion. Consult the two key Ofsted documents that are at this point essential reading:

   ◼ *School Inspection Handbook*. This sets out what inspectors must do and what schools can expect as well as providing guidance for inspectors on making their judgements. It might help to start with pages 27 onwards where there are very clear descriptions of what each grade means in each of the five areas that inspectors make judgements on.[16]

   ◼ *Framework for School Inspection*. This publication summarises the main features of school inspections and is more descriptive; for example, it sets out what to expect if a school fails its inspection.[17]

   Also check the bibliography of this book for Ofsted and other good practice guides.

8. Working with the head teacher, focus on the relevant parts of the *Inspection Handbook* so that you all know what questions to ask – and have evidence that you are asking them.

9. If the school is at risk of failing an inspection, there must be good evidence of very strong 'capacity to improve' – a track record of accurately identifying what needs fixing and then fixing it. Always have case studies available. This may be enough for you to be *sure* that the school doesn't need to fail its inspection in order for standards to rise rapidly, and that your self-evaluation of capacity to improve is accurate. If you are convinced as a school, then you can go on to present the evidence authoritatively to the Ofsted inspectors.

10. Hide nothing.

This extract from a 2012 Ofsted school report demonstrates how governing bodies are judged and can improve in their role in the governance of a school:

The governing body supports the headteacher in securing improvements across the school by challenging weaker practices. The recent restructuring of the governing body with the recruitment of new members has helped to better define the responsibilities of each committee. Governors have received a wide range of relevant training which has equipped them with skills and knowledge essential for performing their duties. The governors visit the school frequently to enable them to collect first-hand information. They have a good understanding of the strengths and weaknesses of the school. They understand data on pupils' progress. Their knowledge of what happens in the school helps them to challenge the school leaders effectively but these efforts are recent and have not had time to make marked improvement on pupils' achievement across the school. Governors fulfil their statutory duties by making sure that the safeguarding and child protection procedures are in place to keep pupils safe. The governors monitor and manage the finances of the school well to ensure that funds are spent on improving resources and the outdoor areas, especially the woodlands, so that they provide rich experiences and better outcomes for pupils. Currently, the governors ensure that the pupil premium is spent on recruiting staff to provide one-to-one support for pupils who require additional support for their learning. In addition, the pupil premium is spent in acquiring educational resources necessary for pupils who are eligible for extra support. However, the achievements of these groups of pupils are still below national averages.

There are two developments you should know about:

1. **Data Dashboard**

   On 27 February 2013, the head of Ofsted, Sir Michael Wilshaw, said:

   > The School Data Dashboard I am launching today raises the stakes. Many governors know their school well already. But for those that don't, there are now no excuses. Inspectors will be very critical of governing bodies who, despite the dashboard, still don't know their school well enough.[18]

   The Data Dashboard really is very easy to use – addictive, even! Why not add a demonstration to your very next meeting and the hyperlink in the minutes?

   The Data Dashboard is available at http://dashboard.ofsted.gov.uk.

2. **Reviews of governance**

When the outcome of an inspection is that a school is judged to require improvement, an external review of governance may be one of the actions a school is required to take, and pay for.

The purpose of the review is to enable schools to move out of the 'requires improvement' category into at least 'good' by helping the governing body to identify priorities for improvement in governance and to provide support on what steps should be taken to achieve those improvements. This review is offered as support to improve and develop governance, and not as an additional inspection.[19]

One of the aims of this book is for you to have the evidence that your governing body does not require this additional support – that you are on the way to 'good' already, and beyond that to 'outstanding'.

Chapter 6

Appointing a new head teacher

This chapter will cover:

■ The entire process from the resignation of your head teacher through to ensuring a smooth transition to the new one

Even if a headship vacancy isn't imminent in your school, reading through the example person specification and the head teacher's job description (Appendices 9 and 10) will give you a good insight into what heads do and what attributes they bring to their work.

Real responsibility: it is governors who appoint the leading professional

The leadership of the head teacher really is as important to the success of the school as everyone says it is:

> Unless we have headteachers who take on the difficult challenges of schools performance and adopt a *no excuses* culture, we are never going to make the improvements we need.
>
> Sir Michael Wilshaw[20]

> The headteacher now monitors and checks that leaders are fulfilling their responsibilities successfully while exploiting opportunities to develop leadership skills still further.[21]

Appointing a new head teacher is one of the occasions when governors visibly fulfil their strategic role. Not surprisingly, this process is very demanding. It doesn't happen often – a governor may have only one or two opportunities to participate during their tenure – and there are no rehearsals, so the pressure is on to get it right first time.

Chapter 6

How head teachers resign

The head teacher will almost always let the chair of governors know they are planning to resign before they make any other announcements. The rest of the governing body will be informed at about the same time as the staff. A long-serving head teacher may indicate to the chair as much as a year ahead that they are either beginning to look for other career opportunities or are retiring.

Teachers, including head teachers, almost invariably give plenty of notice and time their resignation to give a minimum of about a term in which to appoint a replacement. Such a long period can seem curious to governors who may be more familiar with shorter timescales in the private sector, but the process provides a measure of stability for the whole school staff and ensures pupils have continuity. This would be harder to achieve if teachers could come and go every month.

As soon as they have been informed, the governing body can start succession planning, always providing that the head teacher agrees. Indeed, that is almost certainly why the head gave early warning of their intentions, although they may not actually provide a letter of resignation immediately. However, until they do, the head teacher has every right to change their mind. Circumstances can alter – the offer of the post they had accepted may be withdrawn or their family circumstances might mean they are unable to retire after all. The chair will agree with the head teacher what can be done before the letter of resignation arrives. The governing body must not act on the assumption that this will definitely happen.

> I was on the point of writing the letter to take early retirement, when our son, 22, and still living at home, was made redundant, and I thought I had better wait until he had a job again.
>
> Head teacher

Planning – critically important to success

It is part of the etiquette of the teaching profession that outgoing head teachers do not participate in any way in the appointment of their successor. This can be hard for any head teacher: they are the one person who has had right of access to every corner of the premises, who can ask to see any pupil or member of staff, who can contact any governor, parent or guardian and who has had a say in every appointment. As the individual who knows most about the school, it might seem odd that this is the one person not involved in the appointment of a new head teacher.

The reason is that this is another moment when the governors exercise their strategic role and influence the future direction of the school. It may be the opportunity they have been waiting for to lead the school in a new direction.

Planning for a new headship consists of:

- Deciding what professional support is required
- Selecting a group of governors to make the appointment
- Deciding what you are looking for in the new head teacher
- Designing a communications plan – from advertising the post to informing people of the outcome
- Revisiting the vision or mission statement

These are dealt with in turn below.

Deciding what professional support is required

The first port of call is wherever you source your advice and support for personnel matters. It may be a private company, your local authority, your own in-house team or central academy chain team. You may discover you have no choice but to engage the latter and then follow their guidance.

On the other hand, you may find you have the freedom to make and pay for your own arrangements. If so, decide what level of support you need and set a budget accordingly. Don't be surprised if estimates for the highest level of support costs are well over £10,000 for the largest schools.

Within the governing body you will find yourselves in one of the following positions:

- A high level of expertise

  You decide you need only the minimum advice – perhaps designing and placing the advertisement for the post and drawing up the employment contract.

- A high level of confidence and ability to lead and manage the process but limited knowledge of employment practices

  You decide to buy in just enough professional support to cover any gaps and ensure you have someone on hand to advise when the unexpected happens.

- Limited experience

  You decide to buy in the full package, for which there are three main sources:

  - National providers who specialise in head teacher appointments, e.g. the head teacher associations and the *TES* (what used to be the *Times Educational Supplement*)

  - Executive recruitment companies

  - Smaller-scale private sector consultancies and companies

This may be unfamiliar territory because for many years local authorities led or provided expert support for the head teacher appointment process. Schools now have the choice to be creative and use alternatives to tried and tested methods.

Nigel Banister of GMD People sets out the various private sector options:

> *National recruitment businesses use a database to 'marry up' the needs of an employer and a job seeker. If you turn to one of these for help they may well have the ideal candidate they can very quickly offer you. Check that the business has actually met the candidate and they believe them to be suitable for your particular role. Many don't meet candidates as it is time-consuming and therefore costly. They use clever software to 'data mine' CVs they find on the internet, looking for the key words used in your advertisement or job description. Their fee is a percentage of salary of the post. The final figure is always open to negotiation with these types of agencies.*

> *Smaller, locally based recruitment businesses do form better relationships with candidates and tend to offer a more personal service. It is more likely they have met candidates but it may not always be the case. Again, they work in similar ways to the bigger companies with their fee being a percentage of salary.*

> *Executive recruitment businesses only specialise in positions that are paid over a certain salary level, typically £40k, and work in one of two ways. Either they behave as outlined above, or they offer a bespoke service: ensure they advertise specifically for you, meet every candidate who on paper matches your needs and confirm this is the case by using carefully structured competency-based interview questions. They will likely use other tools such as personality profiling and ability testing, all of which are designed to add information to help you make the right recruitment decision.*

Fees for such services may be based on a percentage of salary or be offered as a fixed fee for the service – both are usually negotiable and the latter is referred to as managed recruitment.

Executive search (head hunting) is handled by 'covert' recruiters. They only look for people for you who are not looking for a job. Most recruitment agencies who offer executive search outsource this activity to researchers. Their fees are not usually negotiable and a typical cost for their service is £500 per day with each assignment averaging about six to ten days. They only find candidates who might be interested in talking to you – the rest is up to you.

The best advice when selecting one of these options is to simply use your normal purchasing and contracting procedures. If the providers are local you can invite them to make a presentation. Whatever you choice you make, this source of help is referred to below as an 'external adviser'.

Selecting a group of governors to make the appointment

Choosing which governors to involve is a matter for the chair. Often more people will volunteer than can be used on the day(s) of the interviews. The appointment panel will need to be a balanced group: broadly representative of the governing body and having relevant knowledge and experience to bring to bear. This is unlikely to be an easy choice but offers an opportunity to use the outcomes of any skills audit of the governing body that you have recorded. There is a format for doing this on pp. 33–34.

There are three ways of engaging governors who are not going to be involved on interview day:

1. Show potential applicants around

    Governors can follow up any visit with a phone call to ask for feedback. This can be anonymised, then recorded and passed back to the chair in case any adjustments to visits or the information pack are needed.

2. Form a transition team

    After the appointment, the governors who have been on the interview team will be relieved to take a bit of a break: it is an intensive experience. A transition team will take responsibility from the point at which the post has been accepted to, typically, the end of the first term. Their main task is to ensure that the induction process goes well. The outgoing head teacher will have a lot of knowledge that your transition team can make sure is recorded.

    A transition team will give the governing body the capacity to analyse and meet whatever the new head teacher's needs might be and ensure a smooth start. Almost certainly the new head teacher will have their own ideas about what they need and want, and this will vary depending on whether this is their first or second headship, the characteristics of the school they are coming from and where they are currently living. External appointees may value some local knowledge if they are moving into the area, especially with a young family. A head teacher appointed internally from the school staff will have a wholly different range of transition needs. In any case, the transition will include re-starting the annual appraisal process (see Chapter 4).

3. Exit interview

   Yes, it sounds horribly terminal but will almost certainly be welcomed by the outgoing head teacher.

Deciding what you are looking for in the new head teacher

The key principles are: What are we looking for? and How are we going to find the person who fits most closely? You should use the current School Teachers' Pay and Conditions Document[22] and the head teacher's current job description to draw up a new job description and person specification. Typically it will have a list of *essential* and *desirable* attributes. Applicants will base their application on these documents. At their best, they will enable some potential candidates *not* to proceed to an application because they are clearly not the person you are looking for. Your external adviser will expect to guide this process.

> ### Tip: beware of looking only for the perfect fit ☑
>
> It is tempting to judge everything to be *essential*. The problem can be that you are left with no room for manoeuvre if it puts off good applicants and, of those who do apply, none demonstrate 100% of the essential list. Test each item on the list really thoroughly by asking: Could they *really* not do the job *at all* without this attribute?

Head teacher person specification

Appendix 9 provides an example. It is a guide only – make it your own.

Head teacher job description

As with the person specification, Appendix 10 is a guide only, so make it your own.

Designing the communications plan

This consists of actions based on the outcome of a series of questions:

1. Who do we need to consult with *before* and *during* the entire appointment process?

2. Who do we need to inform about what is happening *before*, *during* and *after* the process?

Actions, as always, must include the following:

- Who?
- How?
- By when?
- Resources required (money, time, space)
- Intended outcome

Designing the appointment process

The next stage is to advertise the post. Create an application pack ready for sending out by post, email or for downloading from your website. Increasingly Facebook pages are used to complement the main school website. If your school doesn't already have a Facebook page, this may be the moment.

Usually, potential applicants will be encouraged to visit the school. This must be carefully considered and must not unfairly advantage or disadvantage any candidate. No one involved in the final appointment process should be involved. On the other hand, it does emphasise that this is a two-way process – you want to give applicants every opportunity to decide whether this is the school where they will be able to thrive as a head teacher.

Your external adviser will provide specific advice about advertising. Ideally, you will attract lots of well-qualified applicants

– and give the right information to enable others to choose *not* to apply.

> We had a potential applicant visit the school. They had never worked outside the centre of London and our school is on a hillside on the edge of a village with glorious views across miles of countryside. He cut the visit short.
>
> 'I'll have to catch the bus and get the train back straight away.'
>
> 'I'm sorry to hear that – may I ask why you feel this is not the school for you?'
>
> 'It's the sight of all those sheep, all those fields, out of every window.'
>
> Secondary head teacher

The external adviser will have a suite of possible questions, activities and ideas for how to schedule the day(s). There are so many variables – they would fill a whole book on their own. However, the key principles are:

1. Use the person specification and job description to design the process.

2. Ensure that everything you do bears scrutiny; especially that you are offering every candidate an equal opportunity to succeed at each stage of the process.

3. Provide briefing and training to any governor who has not participated in appointments before. Equal opportunities training is essential.

4. The perfect person to fill the post probably does not exist. This is why the planning phase is critical as it enables you to be absolutely clear about the essentials and what you are looking for.

5. Sometimes people suggest questions or activities because they think they will be especially challenging and put the candidates under additional pressure. Resist this. The objective is for every applicant to leave the school knowing they have had a fair opportunity to succeed, speaking well of the school and *definitely* disappointed to have been unsuccessful.

Example

Here is a worked example from the person specification to aid your understanding of what process your external adviser may go through.

Person specification:

Demonstrates a level of knowledge and understanding of health, safety, premises and personnel procedures appropriate to their current post and commitment to develop these as required.

This is both essential and only to be assessed at interview.

Process

▨ What questions can we ask that will give every candidate the opportunity to show the extent to which they meet this essential factor?

▨ Do we need to test every element or shall we choose to test one or two and assume the rest are at around the same level?

▨ If one question won't do it, should we have more questions or an activity?

▨ What has worked well in a similar context?

How it might turn out in practice

▨ Drawing one or two examples from your current post, please describe for us what personnel issues you have successfully addressed.

▨ You have had the opportunity to walk round our school. Where do you think the areas of highest risk for the safety of visitors are?

▨ What will you do to be sure you fulfil this part of your headship role successfully?

▨ More and more parents drop their children off and pick them up in cars. We want to halt and then

Contd

reverse this increase. What ideas do you have to achieve this?

This last question will additionally give you some insight into what the candidate brings to the team. They might fire off a dozen thoughts in quick succession or take a moment to reflect and then describe a complete process of getting from where we are now to where we want to be. It could easily be turned into an activity with a written outcome.

The appointment day(s)

Typically, candidates will rotate around a number of question panels and also have time to complete one or more activities in an area set aside for this.

Your external adviser will know how many questions it is possible to ask and answer in 30 minutes (or however long you decide each interview will be) and how much of a gap is needed between sessions to allow for any over-runs.

Finally, it is usual to interview the shortlisted candidates and then to select a smaller number to proceed to the final appointment panel. The criterion must be that after the first round any one of those going forward to the final stage could be appointed to the post: they have demonstrated they meet at least the minimum agreed standard.

Chapter 6

Scoring

All responses need to be assessed and the best way to do this is to make notes and assign a score (e.g. 1-4 or 1-5 if you want to allow a 'not sure' score of 3). It may sound rather mechanistic but it has the benefit of requiring objectivity.

At the end of the process, where one candidate is a long way in front there is unlikely to be much need for further discussion - providing they have passed the minimum threshold.

We made the mistake of not asking two final questions during a deputy head teacher appointment, which is what we had been advised to do! These were:

- Is there any strength of yours that we should know about - one you have not had the opportunity to demonstrate at some point in the process?
- Is there anything we should know about that might affect your ability to fill this post effectively?

We later had to withdraw the offer of the post having discovered that the candidate had not revealed a material fact.

Head teacher

References

References are of increasingly limited value. They are no longer confidential and, in practice, this means they tend to be wholly positive. Confidentiality has also been reduced to almost zero by the use of email for requesting and sending references. You may decide that even a signed hard copy doesn't add anything significant to help you distinguish between applicants. Their use is therefore limited to the very end of the process, just before making the final decision to offer the post.

Having taken reasonable care to check that the reference is genuine, it may simply confirm:

- Factual matters – e.g. dates of service, previous post held, responsibilities of the post, attendance record, any known capability or disciplinary processes.
- Suitability – e.g. does the reference writer know of any reason the candidate may not be suitable?
- Strength of recommendation.

Feedback to candidates

It is good practice to offer telephone feedback to unsuccessful candidates. Whoever does this should agree with the appointment panel two or three positive points to feed back and one or two areas where other candidates gave stronger responses.

Have ready, but do not volunteer, one or two pieces of agreed advice for the candidate's next application. They must be carefully chosen so that they are accurate and not open to challenge – and only shared if the candidate asks for them. If in any doubt, don't offer this advice.

Appendix 1

Becoming a school governor

If you are not already a school governor there are various places to start to find information about the role. These include:

- **SGOSS (formerly School Governors' One-Stop Shop)** – www.sgoss.org.uk

  Highly recommended. This is where you can find out the facts about becoming a school governor, read case studies and start your application. They will also match you to a school nearby – like risk-free internet-dating!

- **Department for Education** – www.education.gov.uk/schools/leadership/governance

  This is a truly comprehensive website. It covers every aspect of education so navigating it can take time, especially if you are unfamiliar with education terminology. School governors are part of school leadership and governance so these are the best areas to start. The site also includes information on becoming a governor.

■ **Local authority**

Your local authority may have a Governors' Services Team who will certainly be pleased to hear from you.

■ **National Governors' Association** – www.nga.org.uk

This association is for governors of state-funded schools.

■ **Association of Governing Bodies of Independent Schools** – http://www.agbis.org.uk/

This association is for governors of private schools.

You will be made welcome by everyone and will be joining other school governors who between them are, according to GovernorLine, 'the largest volunteer workforce in the country, giving freely and generously of their time to help schools achieve the highest standards'.[23]

Appendix 2

A history of education in England and Wales[24]

Summary

▨ A national system of education was established between 1870 and 1944.

▨ Since 1980, schools have become increasingly disparate, especially secondary schools. This includes the ways in which they are led, managed and governed.

▨ Local government's influence is waning. The national government's education minister – the secretary of state for education – had only a handful of matters over which they had decision-making powers before 1980. The number now is over 2,000.

Appendices

Here is an account of the development of state education in England and Wales in five bite-sized chunks.

One

The Christian churches established and ran many schools until the 1870s – which is why numerous schools, especially primary schools, have Church of England (C of E) in their names.

Two

Governing bodies were appointed from the 1870s onwards when the state put in place a national system of education, with schooling available for all children aged 5 to 13, though attendance was not compulsory. School boards were appointed to complete a network of schools. Attendance between the ages of 5 and 10 became compulsory in 1880. The school leaving age was raised to 11 in 1893, 12 in 1899 and 14 in 1921. Most children stayed in one school – an elementary school – from start to finish. Secondary schools were mainly for the children of better-off families, although there were some scholarships. Local education authorities replaced school boards everywhere from 1902.

Three

The 1944 Education Act introduced the system of primary schools, secondary schools and further education colleges that we recognise today – with higher education starting at the age of 18. All pupils transferred to a secondary school at 11. There were different types of secondary school: grammar schools, technical grammar schools and secondary modern schools. Pupils took an examination, the Eleven plus, and were allocated a place on the basis of the results. The school leaving age was raised to 15 in 1947 and 16 in 1972.

Four

In 1965, the government asked local education authorities to prepare proposals to combine the different types of secondary school into one type – secondary comprehensive schools. This led to the end of the Eleven plus almost everywhere.

Five

In 1980 the first Education Act since 1944 was passed and started a transformation of the education system. From about 1985 onwards, the role of local education authorities gradually diminished and the role of central government gradually increased. There have been Acts of Parliament almost every year since 1980, and these have introduced, for example, a national curriculum, national tests at set ages with published results, national standards for teacher training and a national inspection framework, under which all schools are inspected regularly.

The Welsh Government took over responsibility for education in Wales in the late 1990s.

Primary schools remain largely local and comprehensive – most pupils attend their nearest school. Secondary comprehensive schools, however, have been encouraged to become distinctive. Accordingly, parents more often use their right to express a preference, which has introduced an element of competition.

Local education authorities became local authorities in 2005 and from 2010 all schools could become independent and leave local authority supervision. New types of schools have emerged, including free schools, studio schools and university technical colleges. The school leaving age, referred to as the raising of the participation age (RPA) went up to 17 in 2013 and will rise to 18 in 2015.

Appendix 3
Meeting record

Title of group			
Meeting location			
Date and start time		Agreed end time	
Chaired by		Minutes taken by	
Also present			
Purpose of meeting	(if specially convened for a particular purpose, otherwise the title should be enough)		
Matters arising			

Agenda item 1			
Decision	Action	Noted	Referred to _____ for consider-ation
Agenda item 2			
Decision	Action	Noted	Referred to _____ for consider-ation
Agenda item 3			
Decision	Action	Noted	Referred to _____ for consider-ation
Overall outcome of meeting			

Any other business	

Appendix 4

Meeting evaluation checklist

Characteristics	Grade*
Use of time	**Overall**
1. Clear purpose to each agenda item	
2. Keep to time	
3. Concise, clear contributions	
Purposeful mindsets	**Overall**
4. Address challenges	
5. Act: do what we say we will do	
6. Everyone contributes	
7. Everyone actively listens	

---

* 1 - Outstanding; 2 - Good; 3 - Requires improvement; 4 - Inadequate

Characteristics	Grade*
8. Honesty	
Speaking for all those we represent	**Overall**
9. Broad, regular attendance	
10. Equitable participation of all	
Teamwork	**Overall**
11. Share the actions between meetings	
12. Respect people's contributions	

Appendix 5

Twenty key questions for a school governing body to ask itself

Twenty key questions for a school governing body to ask itself[25]	Agree a grade*
Skills: Do we have the right skills within the governing body?	Overall:
1. Have we completed a skills audit of our governing body?	
2. Do we appoint governors on the basis of their skills and do we know how to find people with the necessary skills?	
Effectiveness: Are we as effective as we could be?	Overall:

* 1 - Outstanding; 2 - Good; 3 - Requires improvement; 4 - Inadequate

3. Do we understand our roles and responsibilities?	
4. Do we have a professional clerk and run meetings efficiently?	
5. What is our training and development budget and does every governor receive the support they need to carry out their role effectively?	
6. Do we know about good practice from across the country?	
7. Is the size, composition and committee structure of our governing body conducive to effective working?	
8. Does every member of the governing body make a regular contribution and do we carry out an annual review of the governing body's performance?	

Strategy: Does the school have a clear vision?	Overall:
9. Have we developed long-term aims for the school, with clear priorities, in an ambitious school development plan which is regularly monitored and reviewed?	
10. Does our strategic planning cycle drive the governing body's activities and agenda setting?	
Accountability of the executive: Do we hold the school leaders to account?	Overall:
11. Do we understand the school's performance data well enough to properly hold school leaders to account?	
12. How effective is our performance management of the head teacher?	
13. Are our financial management systems robust and do we ensure best value for money?	

Engagement: Are we properly engaged with our school community, the wider school sector and the outside world?	Overall:
14. How do we listen to and understand our pupils, parents and staff?	
15. How do we report to our parents and local community regularly?	
16. What benefit do we draw from collaboration with other schools and other sectors, locally and nationally?	
Role of chair: Does our chair show strong and effective leadership?	Overall:
17. Do we carry out a regular 360-degree review of the chair's performance?	
18. Do we engage in good succession planning?	
19. Are the chair and committee chairs re-elected each year?	

Impact: Are we having an impact on outcomes for pupils?	Overall:
20. How much has the school improved over the last three years and what has been the governing body's contribution to this?	

Example lesson visit checklist: science department

Focus	Example	Observation	Next steps
Learning environment	Targets, key learning objectives and success criteria on display Labels on items to encourage independence Learning walls – helpful items to assist pupils and reduce the need for them to ask for help Recent and future topics displayed Room set out for easy access		
Who is doing the talking?	Do pupils get the opportunity to be actively involved?		
Is there opportunity for interaction?	Can the pupils work together in pairs, threes or groups?		

	Is the setting appropriate for that style of lesson?	Are pupils sitting in groups? Working in pairs? Can they all see what is going on?			
	Are all pupils on task?	Are they engaged and actively involved in the task?			
	Do the pupils know what they are learning as opposed to what they are doing?	Can they say what they are learning and why?			
	Is there differentia-tion?	Can all pupils access the lesson at their level?			

Focus	Example	Observation	Next steps
Questioning	Does the teacher use questions that challenge all pupils? (e.g. What kinds of questions are being used? Are there probing questions?) Are they open ended? Is any time given for reflection?		
Modelling and demonstrating	Do the pupils know and understand what the work is leading to? Does the teacher demonstrate how to get there in clear easy steps?		
Problem-solving	Are the pupils given opportunities that challenge their thinking? Can they work together to develop solutions?		

Planning	Does the lesson follow the planning? Are layered targets evident in the teaching? Does the teacher audit previous learning? Is there a plenary?		
Support staff	How are they deployed?		
Assessment	Which support staff are with which target group(s) of pupils? What are they focusing on? Are they on task? Are the pupils involved in their own assessments? Do they know what they have to do next to reach the next level?		

Appendix 7
Example learning walk record form

Focus (e.g. discussions with pupils in KS2 to assess attitudes to learning):
Where we went:
Examples we saw of pupils' engagement:
Work scrutiny – evidence of the level of effort we could identify:

Type of work (written, spoken, displays, etc.):

Classroom environment – overall contribution to learning:

Examples of good use of what is around us to aid learning:

Other evidence of pupils' attitudes to learning (e.g. from conversations with pupils, staff, visitors):

Issues and ideas for the future:

Appendix 8

Head teacher's report: suggested headings

Quality of teaching

- How many learning occasions were observed?
- Over what time period?
- What are the percentages of teaching at each of the Ofsted grades and to Ofsted criteria from the most recent set of observations, compared with previous sets?

	Percentage this report	Last report	Previous reports
Outstanding			
Good			
Requires improvement			
Inadequate			

Raising standards
(drawn from the school improvement plan)

■ Who has done what and with what intended impact?

■ To what extent is it working?

■ What will be done next?

Attainment

Attainment will include data from recent pupil assessments to inform the school's understanding of how pupils are doing, and to see the trajectory towards meeting the school's attainment targets.

Issues identified by the last Ofsted inspection

Every Ofsted inspection includes a statement about whether issues identified in the preceding inspection have been successfully addressed. So for each Ofsted issue, the head teacher's report must answer the following questions:

■ Who has done what and with what intended impact? ('Not yet started' is a perfectly sensible response for any lower-priority items.)

■ To what extent is it working?

■ What will be done next?

■ Are we on track to achieve success by the agreed dates?

Specific areas might require more probing questions. For example:

▦ How effective are the arrangements for tracking pupils' progress?

▦ How do staff know their assessments are accurate?

Improving literacy

Literacy is a high priority in all schools. In a primary school, questions to explore standards in literacy might include:

▦ What are the arrangements for choosing books to take home (by key stage)?

▦ How frequently do pupils swap their book for a new book?

▦ What is the range of reading pupils are doing?

▦ How is it recorded?

▦ How is reading commented on by pupils, parents and teachers?

▦ How can governors support this and help parents?

▦ Are standards improving as a result of pupils taking books home?

▦ How do you know?

In a secondary school, questions to probe standards in literacy might include:

▦ What has been the progress of targeted groups of pupils, using agreed measures?

- What are the arrangements for one-to-one and other intensive support?
- How do you know these strategies are working?
- Is literacy modelled and addressed in all departments?
- What have been our successes as a school amongst the following groups:
  - Least able
  - Middle ability
  - Most able
  - Other targeted groups (e.g. pupils with English as an Additional Language, those eligible for the pupil premium, those pupils who arrived at the school with lower than expected literacy skills)
- What needs to be done next to raise overall standards of literacy (by key stage)?

Expenditure of the pupil premium

Spending of the pupil premium must be regularly monitored and evaluated. Questions might include:

- Overall, to what extent is the pupil premium achieving its intended outcomes so far this year? And how does it compare with previous reports?
- What is the allocation of funding by key stage?
- Are there any examples of typical expenditure and intended outcomes?

▨ To what extent are these strategies achieving their intended purpose (by key stage)?

(Note: 'Early evidence' may be all that is available for newly eligible pupils or recently started activities.)

Behaviour and attendance

Summary information, by key stage, should be available on the following matters:

▨ What is the overall judgement on behaviour for learning?
▨ What is the overall judgement on behaviour in unstructured time?
▨ What is the data on unusual episodes of poor behaviour and does it highlight any significant aggravating factors? (Such factors might be bullying, racism, violence, staff on the receiving end, etc)
▨ Any examples of outstanding positive pupil behaviour in any context?
▨ Any recommendations for commendations from the governing body to pupils and staff?

Attendance data

This should be available by key stage and for target groups.

Report on priority areas for improvement

Where the school judges itself to have areas that require improvement or there have been areas judged to require improvement in a previous Ofsted inspection:

- What do you judge the overall sense of urgency amongst the staff to be?
- Are we as governors getting the balance of pressure and support about right?

Capacity to improve

- What are the barriers between where we are now and good *or* now and outstanding?
- What are the really impressive factors helping us to get there?
- What can we, as governors, do more of/less of to assist?

Overall quality of provision

- What great things have been happening to give our pupils an all-round outstanding experience of education since our last meeting?

Two-way communication

- Is there anything your colleagues are keen for us to know about?
- Is there anything that colleagues particularly want to hear about from us?

Future planning

▪ What would you like the focus for governor visits and learning walks with senior staff to be before the next meeting?

▪ What out-of-hours activities can governors visit if they are not available to visit during the working day?

Head teacher person specification

Codes

E = **Essential** Applicant will only be shortlisted if all of these are clearly evidenced.

D = **Desirable** The more the better.

A = **Application** Applicants must include evidence of this either in their letter, their curriculum vitae or on the application form. These will be scored and used for shortlisting.

I = **Interview and selection activities** The interview and other activities will be designed to give opportunities for evidence of this, and may test evidence provided in the application documents.

Experience and qualifications[26]

Element	Essential or desirable	Information provided by
DfE-recognised teaching qualification	E	A
Holds NPQH or equivalent leadership qualification	D	A
Has undertaken learning opportunities relevant to the post, which may include post-graduate qualifications	E	A
Has recent experience of senior management and leadership as a head teacher or deputy head teacher	E	A I
Has compelling evidence of expertise and success in raising standards	E	A I
Has teaching and management experience of the relevant age range of pupils	E	A I

Understands how to bring about change for improvement and shows evidence of having done so successfully	E	A I
Knows how to improve teaching and learning in the classrooms of other staff and shows evidence of having done so	E	A I
Shows evidence of commitment to equality of opportunity for all and of achieving this in practice	E	A I
Has experience of working in an inner-city environment	D	A
Knowledge and experience of management processes including: monitoring, evaluation, data analysis, development planning	E	I
Able to articulate an appropriate process for securing a strategic view of the future needs of the school and how to meet them	E	A I

Element	Essential or desirable	Information provided by
Has worked successfully with governors in a range of contexts and on a range of issues	D	A I
Understands how to manage change and shows evidence of having done so successfully	E	A I
Has knowledge and understanding of planning, monitoring and managing a school's financial resources to achieve intended outcomes	E	A I
Has knowledge and understanding of quality assurance processes, including appraisal	E	A I
Has experience of using pupil-level data to track progress and to set stretching and achievable targets	E	I
Has designed and, where appropriate, led successful staff development	E	A I

Can articulate the principles and practice of curriculum development, including leading staff in this activity	E	I
Understands the principles and practice of inclusive education and can evidence an unshakable commitment to both	E	A I
Knows how to involve parents, carers and the wider community beneficially in the work of the school, including use of school facilities	E	A I
Has experience of working in partnerships with other schools and providers of services to children and young people	D	A
Has full and up-to-date knowledge of both safeguarding and child protection	E	A I
Demonstrates a level of knowledge and understanding of health, safety, premises and personnel procedures appropriate to their current post and commitment to develop these as required	E	I

Personal attributes and dispositions[27]

Criteria	Essential desirable	Information available from
Has resilience and deploys strategies for dealing with both positive and negative stresses at work	E	I
Exemplifies public service values in their behaviours	E	I
Is empathetic – someone a pupil or adult can share concerns and successes with easily	E	A I
Has a sense of fun	D	A I
Demonstrates drive, resolve and determination	E	A I
Enjoys the creative and expressive arts, sports and intellectual activities	D	
Has excellent communication skills	E	A I

Able to assign priorities for self and others – and can take the hard decisions to abandon low-priority activities as well as introduce changes to bring about improvements	E	A
Intellectual flexibility	E	A I
Common sense	E	I

Appendix 10
Head teacher job description

Overall

- Ensure a high quality education for all pupils.
- Provide inspirational leadership and efficient management.

Shape the future

- Formulate, in conjunction with governors, staff, pupils, parents and other stakeholders, the overall vision, values and aims of the school and relevant policies for their implementation.
- Ensure that strategic planning takes account of the diversity, values and experiences of the school and the community it serves.
- Keep the work of the school under continuous review through maintaining a school development plan.

Achieve the task: leadership of learning and teaching

- Undertake a teaching commitment of an appropriate amount.

- Establish creative, responsive and effective learning strategies that are appropriate to the school's context, relevant in today's society and prepare pupils for tomorrow's world.

- Ensure flexible and innovative teaching that is consistent with best practice: challenging, interesting, fun and age appropriate.

- Take a strategic role in the evaluation and deployment of technologies that enhance and extend the learning experiences of pupils.

- Develop a broad, creative and competency-based curriculum which provides the structure for high levels of attainment.

- Ensure a consistent and continuous focus on pupils' achievement, using classroom observations, assessment data and appropriate measures to monitor progress in every pupil's learning.

- Embed systems that accurately identify underperformance, and then enable the design of effective actions to address it in a timely manner.

- Demonstrate and communicate high expectations.

- Set challenging targets for the whole school community.

- Ensure a culture of challenge, support and continuous quality improvement.

Manage the organisation

- Establish and sustain effective structures and systems that manage the school efficiently and effectively on a day-to-day basis.
- Prioritise, plan and organise your own work and that of others.
- Make professional decisions based on well-informed judgements.
- Think creatively to anticipate, avoid and solve problems.

Build the team and develop individuals

- Treat people fairly and with respect.
- Create and maintain an aspirational culture.
- Ensure that the allocation of work to teams and individuals is characterised by reflective planning, well-judged support and careful monitoring and evaluation.
- Build a collaborative learning culture within the school.
- Engage with other schools and providers of services to children and young people.
- Provide adequate learning opportunities for the professional and career development of all staff.

Secure accountability

- Enable all staff and governors to work collaboratively, share knowledge and understanding, celebrate success and accept responsibility for outcomes.

- Ensure that team and individual staff accountabilities are clearly defined, understood and agreed, and are subject to fair and timely review and evaluation.
- Embed a highly effective appraisal process for all staff that complies with current statutory and other guidance.
- Work closely with the governing body and enable it to meet its responsibilities by providing a full range of information, advice and support.
- Provide consistent, clear and accurate reports of each pupil's performance for those with parental responsibility, and in line with current statutory and other appropriate guidance.
- Report regularly on the school's performance to a range of audiences, including staff, governors, pupils, parents, guardians and carers. Reports must enable each audience to draw reliable conclusions in relation to suitable current comparators and over time.

Enhance the community

- Engage with the communities that the school serves in order to contribute to meeting their current and future needs.
- Make the facilities of the school available for appropriate community use.

Appendix 11

Glossary

This section revisits some of the jargon-busting terminology from the introduction. This is because it is designed to function as an alphabetical definition and reference section.

Academy chain. A partnership between two or more academies. There is no fixed pattern – some are all primary, some all secondary, others a mixture – and there are both national and local chains. There are three main models:

1. Multi-academy trust: Academies join together to become one legal entity governed by one trust, with one governing body, board of directors or trustees.

2. Umbrella trust: This is where a group of individual academies sets up an overarching trust to provide shared governance and enable enhanced collaboration.

3. Collaboration: The academies simply agree to work together.

Academy sponsor. An organisation that works in partnership with one or more schools: in the academy programme prior to 2010, sponsors worked only with schools that were judged by Ofsted to be providing an inadequate education. Since 2010 there has been more flexibility.

Achievement. The progress and success of a pupil in their learning.

Action plan. This is helpful in addressing an urgent, complex matter thoroughly. It should be created by whoever 'owns' the issue – the school staff or the governing body. For example, reviewing pupil safety at the start of the school day may become urgent if there is a 'near miss' and a pupil narrowly escapes injury whilst their parent is dropping them off. An action plan contains who will do what, by when and with what resources. In addition, it will show priorities: who will carry the can if the actions do not happen, how success will be measured and milestones. Where necessary, it will show where the start of one set of actions is dependent on actions by others. The school improvement plan needs only a brief modification – a reference to the issue and where the action plan can be found.

Appraisal. This is the compulsory annual judgement about how each teacher is doing. There are DfE regulations and a model policy. The head teacher is appraised by the governing body which has to employ an external adviser as part of the process. It is widely regarded as best practice for all support staff to have an annual review. Appraisal, particularly formal observations of a member of staff whilst they work, is an area that requires strict adherence to the school's policy. Staff associations are always vigilant to ensure appraisals are fair and objective, especially where pay increases depend on a positive outcome. Some staff find formal observations negatively stressful and are keen to ensure that the number of observations is kept to the minimum necessary. Others find it positively stressful – they find it demanding but welcome the opportunity to receive constructive feedback and advice about areas to improve.

Attainment. The standard of pupils' work as shown by test and examination results and in lessons.

Attainment target. In state schools, these are set for every pupil for the end of each key stage – that is, at ages 7, 11, 14 and 16. School targets are built from these and are necessary because attainment test and examination results form the basis of the published performance tables. Beyond the statutory minimum, each school decides what other targets to set.

Authorised absence. This is when a pupil's absence from school has been formally agreed.

Behaviour support plan. Pupils whose behaviour is difficult (i.e. their progress is seriously slowed by what they say and do) will have a behaviour support plan. Their conduct will almost certainly affect the progress of other pupils and also increase the workload of staff. The plan sets out the local arrangements for how the pupil will be supported to improve.

Capability procedures. Governing bodies must have a procedure for dealing with staff whose work performance starts to fall below the standard expected. There is a model DfE capability policy and an obvious link to appraisal. This is an area where policies and procedures must be up to date and represent best practice. Governors should have complete confidence that this is the case well before they are needed: this is amongst the most demanding of personnel activities for everyone involved. If the person concerned is a member of a union, they will consult their union representative for advice and support. If not, they may pay for legal representation. When capability processes start, everyone will be aware that one possible outcome is the dismissal of the member of staff. Governors will be involved and must be prepared for this eventuality.

Capacity to improve. The proven ability of the school to continue improving. Ofsted inspectors base this judgement on what the school has accomplished so far and on the quality of its systems to maintain improvement. This definition is given at the end of every inspection report in the list of terminology inspectors use. Governors evidence their role in this process in the minutes of their meetings.

Capital expenditure. The DfE and local authorities provide grants for spending on assets that, in the public sector, are defined as 'assets above a certain threshold which are expected to be used for a period of at least one year.'[28] The DfE threshold for 2012 is £2,500. Generally, capital expenditure comprises the purchase of land, buildings, computers, machinery and other expensive equipment. Other expenditure is referred to as revenue (e.g. salaries, consumables, taxes).

Children's trusts. Local partnerships of providers of services to children, young people and families. The Children Act 2004 includes a duty for some services to cooperate. This includes schools. Others participate voluntarily.

Cluster. A group of schools in a geographical area which choose to work together to raise standards for pupils and widen educational provision for the local community. Often, especially in rural areas, a cluster comprises primaries and the secondary to which the pupils usually transfer.

Collaboration. Two or more governing bodies working together through, for example, meetings or joint committees.

Core subjects. Subjects which all pupils must study at every key stage.

CRB check (criminal records check). The Criminal Records Bureau recently merged with the Independent Safeguarding Authority to become the Disclosure and Barring Service. Adults who have regular contact with children, young people and/or vulnerable adults will be asked to apply for a DBS check by the school or service provider.

Delegated authority. When a body or a person gives authority to others to take decisions. Governing bodies delegate most matters to the head teacher. The main power it cannot hand over is approving the annual budget plan.

Department for Education (DfE). This is the UK government department responsible for issues relating to young people (up to the age of 19) in England, such as education and child protection.

Disclosure and Barring Service (DBS). In 2012 the Criminal Records Bureau (CRB) and the Independent Safeguarding Authority (ISA) merged to create the DBS. It discloses criminal record information and makes barring decisions for England, Wales and Northern Ireland. It is illegal for a school to knowingly employ a person barred from working with children.

Drop-in. School leaders need to know how things are going anywhere in the school at any time, primarily in classrooms. A drop-in visit – up to around 15 minutes – can have a particular purpose. It may be part of a learning walk; if so, staff will know a visit is likely. A very brief visit can be unannounced and is just part of the normal finding out about how things are going or to follow up on the effectiveness of some action the leader has taken. Any visit that is part of **Appraisal** is an **Observation**; that is, evidence-collecting as part of this formal activity.

Early Years Foundation Stage (EYFS). The major change in 21st century education has been the development of statutory frameworks for the Early Years (ages 0–5). There are now pre-school places for every parent who wants one for their child. School is compulsory only from the term following the child's fifth birthday – unchanged since the 19th century. Some local authorities fund places in nursery schools and primary schools for children younger than this. EYFS provision other than in schools is called a setting and may include children's centres, childminders or voluntary pre-school groups.

Exclusion. This is when a head teacher forbids a pupil from entering school premises for a disciplinary reason. It can be temporary or permanent. Governors are involved if the parent (or student if over 16) appeals against the head's decision.

Extended services. From 2005 onwards, schools were expected to develop a range of additional services and activities. These are not all necessarily organised by the school; instead schools 'signpost' where the services or activities can be found. For example: community access to the school's facilities; support for parents to develop their parenting skills; swift and easy access to providers of support when a pupil needs it; childcare facilities from 8 a.m. to 6 p.m.; or a menu of out-of-school activities for pupils.

Federation. Two or more schools which work together either in an informal arrangement – often called a 'soft federation' – or are formally linked through shared leadership and governance, whilst maintaining an individual character and separate legal identities.

Fischer Family Trust (FFT). This is a charity which provides data for schools to help staff set targets for individual pupils and groups of pupils and then compare outcomes with other schools. When schools say they are using FFTD as the benchmark, it means they are using as their comparison FFT-generated estimates of what pupils *could* achieve if their school were amongst the top 25% of all schools nationally. FFTA is what the bottom 25% of schools are achieving nationally.

Formula funding. All schools receive their funds according to a formula. The most important factor is the number of pupils. School funding deserves a whole book to itself – it is something your head teacher and bursar will be experts in, and so will the governors who serve on whichever of your committees deals with finance. The main element will be the number of pupils in an age group multiplied by £X. This will be the amount allocated to the school. The age-weighted pupil unit (£X) changes annually and varies from one local authority area to another. All publicly funded schools use the same formula in a local authority area for this main element of the school budget. There will be variations in other areas of the budget depending on the status (academy, community school, etc.) and age range of the school. In time there is an intention to move to a national formula.

Framework. This is the basic structure within which a school – or any system – operates.

Further education (FE). A college alternative to a school-based sixth form or sixth-form college. An FE college offers a range of flexible, employment related courses for 16–18-year-olds and adults, full time and part time, and includes courses offered in sixth forms. Part-time courses are offered for some 14–16-year-olds who also attend a school. Tertiary colleges offer a complete range of sixth form and further education college courses. Some FE colleges specialise (e.g. horticulture, agriculture, higher education courses). Others make formal partnerships to lead studio schools or work with academies.

Head teacher's report. Governing bodies normally request a report at each of their full meetings. It is the key document in the process of holding the head teacher to account. Accordingly, it is for the governing body to take the lead in what it contains. It figures high on the list of documents Ofsted inspectors read when they are inspecting a school. Inspectors give great weight to it when they are undertaking a monitoring visit after an inspection where the outcome was anything other than 'good' or 'outstanding' overall.

Higher education. The university sector.

Higher level teaching assistant (HLTA). This is a set of standards that head teachers can use to assess whether a teaching assistant is ready to take on a greater role in leading learning. The word 'teach' is only used formally for teachers but an HLTA will work with small groups and advance pupils' learning in whole groups when their assigned teacher is not present. It is a logical step towards a member of staff deciding to work towards **Qualified teacher status**.

Home–school agreement. All publicly-funded schools, including academies, are required to publish a home–school agreement, drawn up in consultation with parents. It includes the school's aims and values, what the school expects of pupils and parents and what parents can expect of the school. It should pretty much be a statement of the obvious and not be contentious.

Parents cannot be required to sign anything, but it is good practice to invite them to sign a declaration that they understand and accept the agreement. It is also good practice for the governing body to ask the head teacher how many parents sign and what the barriers to achieving 100% sign-up are. Governors should also know to what extent the home–school agreement is contributing to the school achieving its aims.

Impact The actual difference made by an action or intervention. Too often, this is interpreted as *What has changed.* The best way to identify the impact of an action is to ask three questions:

1. Who has benefited?

2. In what ways?

3. By how much?

Institute for Learning (IfL). This is the independent professional body for teachers, tutors, trainers and student teachers in the **Further education** sector.

Interim executive board (IEB). There are circumstances when a school's governing body loses its powers and is replaced by a small group, an IEB, whose task is to bring about rapid improvements and then ensure a smooth transition of the school back to normal governance arrangements.

Key stage (KS). These are used in order to make comparisons of pupils' attainment and progress through their schooling. Measurements are made at the end of each stage:

Early Years Foundation Stage (0–5)

Key Stage 1   (5–7)

Key Stage 2   (7–11)

Key Stage 3   (11–14)

Key Stage 4   (14–16)

Schools sometimes refer to their sixth form as Key Stage 5.

Leadership and management. The contribution of the head teacher, all staff with leadership responsibilities and the governing body in identifying school priorities, directing and motivating staff and running the school.

Learning. How well pupils acquire knowledge, develop their understanding, learn and practise skills and improve their competence as learners.

Learning walk. This is a formal, planned walk through as much of the school as possible – or as much as is necessary for the purpose of the walk – with particular aims in mind. Senior staff will use learning walks regularly to inform their evaluation of the quality of provision with sound evidence and will use an agreed format for recording their observations and judgements.

Looked-after child. These are children and young people for whom, for a range of reasons, the local authority is acting as the parent on a long- or short-term basis. There is a specific legal definition but the important matter for governors is that this group generally do less well at school than they should and could. We are all responsible for keeping a friendly eye on them. All head teachers will know which pupils are looked after at any one time and will have ready access to information on how they are doing. Governors should expect to ask about this group of children regularly.

National curriculum. This is a framework of 12 subjects, divided into Key Stages 1, 2 and 3. It is only compulsory in schools in England and only in local authority schools. A tightly defined national curriculum was introduced in the 1980s; before that schools were responsible for developing their own curriculum. The national curriculum is more flexible now, once again giving schools a measure of choice. Private schools and academies do not have to follow the national curriculum.

Newly qualified teacher (NQT). A teacher who has been qualified to teach for less than a year.

Observation. A formal occasion when a member of staff observes a colleague teaching, makes a judgement on its quality, keeps a record and gives feedback to the teacher. This is not a term which governors should use for any other activity: there are so few jobs where this happens that it is easy to overlook how it might generate stress. This can be a sensitive matter, especially in a school where teaching is not already 'good' overall and teachers are focusing on reaching this standard.

Ofqual. The Office of the Qualifications and Examinations Regulator is the body responsible for regulating examinations and the national curriculum tests.

Ofsted. The Office for Standards in Education, Children's Services and Skills inspects or regulates, amongst others, state and independent schools, teacher training providers and FE and HE colleges in England.

Open enrolment. This is the statutory requirement for schools to admit up to the **published admissions number**, which is the fixed number of pupils in the intake year group as published by the admission authority, usually the local authority.

Overall effectiveness. Ofsted inspectors use the following judgements to reach a view about effectiveness:

- Capacity to improve
- Outcomes for individual pupils and groups of pupils
- The quality of teaching
- The extent to which the curriculum meets pupils' needs
- The effectiveness of care, guidance and support

Parental responsibility. There is simply no way round reproducing the entry from the Department for Education's guide for governors: 'Parental responsibility means all the rights, duties, powers, responsibilities and authority that a parent of a child has by law.' It is a technical term and schools will be very familiar with what it means in practice. For more detail – read on!

More than one person may have parental responsibility for the same child at the same time, and a person does not cease to have such responsibility solely because some other person subsequently also acquires it. Both parents have parental responsibility if they were married to each other at the time of the child's birth, although they may have since separated or divorced. If the child's parents were not married at the time of the birth, the mother has parental responsibility for the child, and the father is able to acquire parental responsibility for the child if he: marries the mother of the child; enters into a parental responsibility agreement with the mother; registers the child's birth jointly with the mother (effective from 1 December 2003, but not retrospective); or applies to the court for a parental responsibility order. A residence order confers parental responsibility on the holder for the duration of the order. Parental responsibility passes to the adopter when an adoption order is made. Although a care order confers parental responsibility on an LA [Local Authority], the LA will not be treated as a parent for certain purposes under the Education Acts.[29]

So, for example, it will be the person with whom the child lives who will receive letters from the school, sign consent forms or have a vote to elect parent governors – not someone who works for the local authority.

Parent View. Ofsted inspectors want to understand what parents think of a school. This part of their website is available to parents to record their opinions. Whilst we can reasonably assume that most parents have access to the internet and are confident users, it may be a good idea to know the extent to which this is true and make arrangements to support parents where they want it. For example, making a computer available at parents' evenings, having someone on hand to help a less confident parent or one with special needs, briefing your local library or providing a display poster.

Parents. Families can be complicated! Parents are partners with the school in the education of their children, and therefore there is a great deal of guidance about developing this relationship for the benefit of the child. Schools have developed expertise in this area over many years. In education law, a parent is any person who has parental responsibility, so that will also include a local authority. The legal definition is: 'all natural parents, whether married or not; any person who, although not a natural parent, has care of a child or young person'.[30] 'Any person' refers to the adult(s) the child lives with and who looks after them, whatever their relationship. Schools will, for example, have records to show who to send additional reports to if the natural parent is not currently living with their child.

Peripatetic teacher. Teachers of musical instruments are often affectionately referred to as 'peris': they travel from school to school and have sessions with pupils on a one-to-one or group basis. It is a matter for the school whether this tuition is paid for by the parents or the school, so governors will have a policy on this. It is a good example of the role governors play – the decision whether to charge parents or not will be driven by their vision and aims for the school, the relative importance of this activity when considering all the demands on the school budget and other contextual factors like the history and traditions of the school and what other arrangements are available to parents and pupils.

Less frequently, a school may engage a peripatetic teacher for other purposes – to address a pupil's very specific special education needs, coach a sports team, teach a drama group or provide one-to-one support for a pupil who has fallen behind their peers. As with music lessons, it is a matter for the school and/or governors to decide whether this tuition is paid for by parents or the school.

Persistent absence/absentee (PA). There is a strong correlation between high levels of pupil attendance and how well that pupil does at school. Schools must record attendance data and Ofsted inspectors always look at it. The definition of PA is 15%: that is, pupils should be present for more than 85% of sessions. There are two sessions in a school day and typically 190 days in a school year. This threshold is used so that interventions can be monitored (What actions?) and evaluated (How well are they working?) and compared with other schools locally and nationally.

This is a group of pupils whose educational progress governors will monitor, usually via the **head teacher's report**. It is far better to spot a trend and take early action (a pupil whose attendance is falling but has not yet dropped below 85%) than start to act when the figure reaches the threshold but then continues to fall. The less frequently a pupil is in school the more likely it is that they will not achieve, and the more difficult it is to then reverse the trend. Again, schools have a lot of experience in examining attendance data and taking action. Overall attendance is typically around 95%.

Phonics. A method of teaching reading which is based on linking sounds in the spoken language with their corresponding letter or letter combinations.

Plan. A structured way of achieving what we want to achieve as a school – the minimum must be a list of actions, who will do them and by when.

Plenary. This is the final phase of a lesson when a teacher will work with pupils to secure the learning, make a judgement about progress, agree any necessary adjustments to homework tasks and begin to plan the next lesson.

Policy. A way of doing things which has been formally agreed and which everyone must follow.

Private finance initiative (PFI). Introduced in 1995, this is a way of funding school buildings using private money which is then repaid by the school over a long period, like a mortgage on a house. The buildings and other facilities are usually managed by the organisation that raised the money, so the relationship with the school is like that between landlord and tenant.

Progress. The rate at which pupils are learning in lessons and over longer periods of time. It is often measured by comparing the pupils' attainment at the end of a key stage with their attainment when they started.

Published admissions number (PAN). The fixed number of pupils in the intake year group as published by the admission authority, usually the local authority.

Pupil premium. This is an additional fixed sum of money paid to a school for each pupil known to be eligible for free school meals, for the children of parents serving in the armed forces and for pupils in the care of the local authority – **looked-after children**. Schools are expected to target this money at improving the quality of provision for each of the eligible pupils and evaluate accurately the extent to which this has been achieved. Governors must ensure this is part of the data set in the **head teacher's report** to the governing body.

Pupil referral unit (PRU). A school which provides education for pupils who have been excluded (expelled) from a mainstream school or who are unable to attend a mainstream school for some other reason (e.g. ill health). PRUs can be independent or community schools.

Qualified teacher status (QTS). Someone with QTS can teach school pupils of any age. Teachers who trained in a further education college are members of the **Institute for Learning**, and have qualified teacher learning and skills status (QTLS), and can also teach in schools.

Quorum. This is the number of governors who must be present at a meeting to make it an official meeting with valid decisions.

RAISEonline. Reporting and Analysis for Improvement through School Self-Evaluation is provided online by Ofsted and the Department for Education. All national curriculum test and examination results are included, alongside data on localities. It is a vast online database: schools can drill down through the data to individual pupil level and make what appears to be an infinite choice of what to compare with what and over what time period. If you need to know what percentage of your pupils come from households in a particular income bracket compared with similar-sized schools nationally and locally, then this is the place! The site can only be accessed with a secure password. A useful tip to start with is to ask the data person in your school to show you around the system – they will give you an overview of what is available and what the leadership team has selected as the items they want to see regularly. This may take more than one session. After that, you can start framing the questions you want to see the answers to. Schools also use **Fischer Family Trust** information.

Reports. We all remember these! Every head teacher is required to provide an annual written report on each pupil's educational achievements. Not surprisingly, this is a task they always delegate to the people who know the pupils best – their teachers.

Standard Assessment Tests (SATs). National curriculum assessments used at the end of Key Stages 1 and 2 (ages 7 and 11).

Self-evaluation form (SEF). The Ofsted Inspection Schedule is a powerful mechanism used by the government of the day to influence schools. For many years, Ofsted expected schools to 'inspect themselves' and have the evidence to show that they had done so and that this was raising standards. Ofsted produced a SEF on its website which schools could use and keep up to date but that was 'locked' when the date of the school inspection was announced. The vast majority of schools still regard having a SEF as a requirement. There are two common criticisms of SEFs: there is often too much description of *what we are doing* and not enough judgements about *whether it is working.* A governing body should also model self-evaluation behaviour by carrying out an annual review.

Standards and Testing Agency (STA). The organisation responsible for the development and delivery of all statutory assessments from the Early Years to the end of Key Stage 3.

Standing Advisory Council on Religious Education (SACRE). An independent body which considers the provision of religious education in a local authority area. It is comprised of representatives of the local authority, teaching profession and church/faith groups.

Strategy and strategic leadership. The overall way in which we are going to achieve what we want to accomplish in the medium to long term – it is where the leadership is leading us and includes the planning to get us there.

Teaching Agency. Now the National College for Teaching and Leadership. Part of the Department for Education which is responsible for initial teacher training and for supporting the recruitment and professional development of the Early Years workforce.

Trusts. A charitable (not-for-profit) organisation that – in the context of schools – is the overarching body that will usually have the power to identify and appoint governors for the schools that are within the trust.

Unauthorised absence. This is when a pupil is absent from school without the school's permission. The abbreviation PA (**persistent absence/absentee**) is used to identify one group of pupils that governors need to know about – what the school is doing to improve their attendance and whether it is working.

Voluntary. This word is used a lot in relation to children and young people: it simply means an organisation that is not established by legislation – it doesn't *have* to exist. Thus charities are voluntary bodies; so are faith organisations and local youth groups run by community volunteers. Because volunteers often gift their time to voluntary organisations, there can be some confusion because these bodies may also have paid employees, often on similar pay and conditions as if they were in the public or private sector. Governors are usually volunteers. An academy trust is a voluntary body that will have paid employees.

Voluntary aided (VA) or **voluntary controlled (VC).** These are schools set up by a voluntary body – often the Church of England because Christian organisations provided most of the education until the 1870s. VA schools are *largely* funded by their local authority; VC schools are *wholly* funded by the local authority. In any school with 'voluntary' in the description of its legal status, the whole matter of who owns what, and who employs the staff, is complex and may be changing, so your head teacher will be the person to ask about the current position.

Warning notice. This is the last entry – and I hope that you never see one of these. Local authorities have a duty to ensure the quality of provision of state education for the children and young people in their area. They are also responsible for the well-being of *all* children and young people whose home is in the geographic area, irrespective of where they are schooled, including those educated in private schools and at home. A local authority has the power to write to the governing body if it has any concerns about the performance of the school (e.g. examination and test results), the leadership or management of the school and pupil or staff safety. This letter constitutes a warning notice, often referred to as a 'formal warning'. The governing body will be expected to address any concerns raised as a matter of urgency.

Endnotes

1. There is an additional vocabulary list in Appendix 11.

2. DfE, Governing Body: An Overview (April 2012). Available at: http://www.education.gov.uk/schools/ leadership/governance/becomingagovernor/ rolesandresponsibilities/a0056658/governing-body-an-overview (accessed 29 January 2013).

3. DfE, *The Governors' Guide to the Law* (May 2012). Available at: http://media.education.gov.uk/assets/files/ pdf/g/governors%20guide%20may%202012.pdf (accessed 29 January 2013).

4. Ofsted, *The Framework for School Inspection* (December 2012). Ref: 120100. Available at: http://www.ofsted.gov. uk/resources/framework-for-school-inspection/ (accessed 29 January 2013), p. 19.

5. 'Chain' is used to mean any sort of formal arrangement, including clusters, federations, academy sponsors, local authority, private, faith and other not-for-profit providers.

6. DfE, *Policies and Other Documents that Governing Bodies and Proprietors Are Required to Have by Law* (October 2012). Available at: http://media.education.gov.uk/assets/files/ pdf/s/statutory%20policies%20for%20schools-%2010%20 october%202012.pdf (accessed 29 January 2013).

7. Ofsted, *The Evaluation Schedule for the Inspection of Maintained Schools and Academies* (2012). Ref: 090098, p. 20.

8. DfE, *Teacher Appraisal and Capability: A Model Policy for Schools* (May 2012). Available at: http://media.education. gov.uk/assets/files/pdf/m/model%20policy%20rev%20 17%20may%20branded.pdf (accessed 29 January 2013).

9. DfE, *Teachers' Standards* (September 2012). Available at: http://media.education.gov.uk/assets/files/pdf/t/ teachers%20standards%20information.pdf (accessed 29 January 2013).

10. DfES, *National Standards for Headteachers* (October 2004). Available at: https://www.education.gov.uk/publications/ standard/publicationDetail/Page1/DFES-0083-2004 (accessed 29 January 2013).

11. Ofsted, *School Inspection Handbook* (December 2012). Ref: 120101. Available at: http://www.ofsted.gov.uk/resources/ school-inspection-handbook/ (accessed 29 January 2013), p. 43.

12. Ofsted, *Local Authorities and Home Education* (June 2010). Ref: 090267. Available at: www.ofsted.gov.uk/resources/

local-authorities-and-home-education (accessed 29 January 2013).

13. Ofsted was established in 1992 in England. Wales, Scotland and Northern Ireland developed their own versions, as did the private education sector.

14. It is as yet unclear what the mechanism will be for removing school places where there are more places than pupils, now that local authorities have fewer schools of their own that they can close, merge or shrink.

15. HC Select Committee on Education, *The Role and Performance of Ofsted – Second Report* (23 March 2011). Available at: http://www.publications.parliament.uk/pa/cm201011/cmselect/cmeduc/570/57002.htm (accessed 29 January 2013), para. 91.

16. Ofsted, *School Inspection Handbook*.

17. Ofsted, *The Framework for School Inspection*.

18. 'Schools to Get Annual Report Cards', *The Guardian* (27 February 2013). Available at http://www.guardian.co.uk/education/2013/feb/27/schools-get-annual-report-cards (accessed 11 June 2013).

19. DfE/National College for Teaching and Leadership, Review of Governance (2013). Available at http://www.education.gov.uk/nationalcollege/review-of-governance (accessed 11 June 2013).

20. Ofsted, 'High Expectation, No Excuses – Sir Michael Wilshaw HMCI Outlines Changes to Ofsted Inspection in Drive to Deliver a Good Education For All' (press release, 9 February 2012). Ref: NR2012-08. Available at: http://www.ofsted.gov.uk/news/high-expectation-no-excuses-sir-michael-wilshaw-hmci-outlines-changes-ofsted-inspection-drive-delive (accessed 29 January 2013).

21. Ofsted, *Getting to Good: How Headteachers Achieve Success* (September 2012). Ref: 120167. Available at: http://www.ofsted.gov.uk/resources/getting-good-how-headteachers-achieve-success/ (accessed 29 January 2013), p. 20.

22. DfE, *School Teachers' Pay and Conditions Document 2012* (August 2012). Ref: DFE-00091-2012. Available at: http://www.education.gov.uk/schools/careers/payandpensions/a0064179/school-teachers-pay-and-conditions-document-2011 (accessed 29 January 2013).

23. See http://www.education.gov.uk/governorline (accessed 29 January 2013).

24. Education in Scotland and Northern Ireland developed in a similar but distinctive way.

25. Published on 9 July 2012 at the Summer Reception of the All Party Parliamentary Group on Education Governance and Leadership. Available at: http://www.nga.org.uk/getattachment/News/NGA-News/

APPG-20-Questions/20-questions-for-the-GB-v2-July-2012.pdf.aspx (accessed 29 January 2013). I have added the second column and scoring grid.

26. However, note Keith Grint's warning that 'the critical issue cannot simply be experience, but what is learned through experience': 'Learning to Lead: Can Aristotle Help Us Find the Road to Wisdom?', *Leadership* 3(2) (2007): 231–232.

27. According to Jonathan Doh, 'leadership comprises skills, perspectives and dispositions': 'Can Leadership Be Taught? Perspective from Management Educators', *Academy of Management Learning and Education* 2(1) (2003): 59.

28. HM Treasury, Managing Public Money (May 2012). Available at: http://www.hm-treasury.gov.uk/psr_mpm_index.htm (accessed 29 January 2013).

29. DfE, *The Governors' Guide to the Law*, pp. 200–201.

30. Education Act 1996, Section 576.

Bibliography and further reading

The Department for Education and Ofsted are the main sources of information.

The DfE website is a very helpful and extensive source of information. It also includes the national archive of resources and information from the initiatives and organisations that used to be part of the education system but no longer exist, or have changed their name or where they are based. For example, if you want to find resources which were used by the National Literacy and Numeracy Strategies, you can search for them here. Such resources have been archived because they still have value.

Adamson, S. (ed.) (2012). *The School Governors' Yearbook*. Norwich: Adamson Publishing.

All Party Parliamentary Group on Education Governance and Leadership (2012). Effective Governance for Good Schools: Twenty Key Questions for a School Governing Body to Ask Itself. Available at: http://www.nga.org.uk/getattachment/ News/NGA-News/APPG-20-Questions/20-questions-for-the- GB-v2-July-2012.pdf.aspx (accessed 29 January 2013).

Beere, J. (2012). *The Perfect Ofsted Inspection*. Carmarthen: Crown House Publishing.

Burnham, L. (2011). *Supporting Teaching and Learning in Schools (Secondary)*. Oxford: Heinemann.

Burnham, L. and Baker, B. (2010). *Level 3 Diploma. Supporting Teaching and Learning in Schools (Primary), Candidate Handbook*. Oxford: Heinemann.

Coleman, A. (2006). *Collaborative Leadership in Extended Schools*. Nottingham: NCSL.

DfE (2012). 'Governing Body: An Overview' (April). Available at: http://www.education.gov.uk/schools/leadership/governance/becomingagovernor/rolesandresponsibilities/a0056658/governing-body-an-overview/ (accessed 29 January 2013).

DfE (2012). Policies and Other Documents that Governing Bodies and Proprietors are Required to Have by Law (October). Available at: http://media.education.gov.uk/assets/files/pdf/s/statutory%20policies%20for%20schools-%2010%20october%202012.pdf (accessed 29 January 2013).

DfE (2012). *School Teachers' Pay and Conditions Document 2012* (August). Ref: DFE-00091-2012. Available at: http://www.education.gov.uk/schools/careers/payandpensions/a0064179/school-teachers-pay-and-conditions-document-2011 (accessed 29 January 2013).

DfE (2012). *Teacher Appraisal and Capability: A Model Policy for Schools* (May). Ref: DfE v1.2 17/05/2012. Available at: http://media.education.gov.uk/assets/files/pdf/m/model%20policy%20rev%2017%20may%20branded.pdf (accessed 29 January 2013).

DfE (2012). *Teachers' Standards* (September). Available at: http://media.education.gov.uk/assets/files/pdf/t/teachers%20 standards%20information.pdf (accessed 29 January 2013).

DfE (2012). *The Governors' Guide to the Law* (May). Available at: http://media.education.gov.uk/assets/files/pdf/g/ governors%20guide%20may%202012.pdf/ (accessed 29 January 2013).

DfE/National College for Teaching and Leadership, Review of Governance (2013). Available at http://www.education.gov. uk/nationalcollege/review-of-governance (accessed 11 June 2013).

DfES (2004). *National Standards for Headteachers* (October). Ref: DfES/0083/2004. Available at: https://www.education. gov.uk/publications/standard/publicationDetail/Page1/DFES-0083-2004 (accessed 29 January 2013).

Doh, J. (2003). 'Can Leadership Be Taught? Perspective from Management Educators', *Academy of Management Learning and Education* 2(1): 55–67. Available at: http://www.ioe.stir.ac.uk/ documents/MTEP16Reader-Doh.pdf (accessed 29 January 2013).

Grint, K. (2007). 'Learning to Lead: Can Aristotle Help Us Find the Road to Wisdom?', *Leadership* 3(2): 231–246.

HC Select Committee on Education (2011). The Role and Performance of Ofsted – Second Report (23 March). Available at: http://www.publications.parliament.uk/pa/cm201011/ cmselect/cmeduc/570/57002.htm (accessed 29 January 2013).

HM Treasury (2012). *Managing Public Money* (May). Available at: http://www.hm-treasury.gov.uk/psr_mpm_index.htm (accessed 29 January 2013).

Joseph, J. (2000). *Stress Free Teaching: A Practical Guide to Tackling Stress in Teaching, Lecturing and Tutoring.* London: Kogan Page.

Jozwiak, G. (2012). 'Regional Ofsted Directors to Inspect Councils that Fail to Improve Schools', Children and Young People Now (28 November). Available at: http://www.cypnow.co.uk/cyp/news/1075505/regional-ofsted-directors-inspect-councils-fail-improve-schools (accessed 29 January 2013).

Kamen, T. (2011). *Teaching Assistant's Handbook: Level 3. Supporting Teaching and Learning in Schools.* London: Hodder Education.

Kirkham, S. (2012). 'Bird's Eye View – Don't Fall Prey to the Latest Ofsted Inspections'. *Leader* 67: 14–16.

McKimm, J. and Phillips, K. (eds) (2009). *Leadership and Management in Integrated Services.* Exeter: Learning Matters.

Ofsted (2010). *Local Authorities and Home Education* (June). Ref: 090267. Available at: www.ofsted.gov.uk/resources/local-authorities-and-home-education (accessed 29 January 2013).

Ofsted (2011). *School Governance: Learning from the Best* (May). Ref: 100238. Available at: www.ofsted.gov.uk/resources/school-governance (accessed 29 January 2013).

Ofsted (2012). 'High Expectation, No Excuses – Sir Michael Wilshaw HMCI Outlines Changes to Ofsted Inspection in

Drive to Deliver a Good Education For All' (press release, 9 February). Ref: NR2012-08. Available at: http://www.ofsted. gov.uk/news/high-expectation-no-excuses-sir-michael-wilshaw-hmci-outlines-changes-ofsted-inspection-drive-delive (accessed 29 January 2013).

Ofsted (2012). *Getting to Good: How Headteachers Achieve Success* (September). Ref: 120167. Available at: http://www.ofsted. gov.uk/resources/getting-good-how-headteachers-achieve-success/ (accessed 29 January 2013).

Ofsted (2012). *The Framework for School Inspection* (December). Ref: 120100. Available at: http://www.ofsted.gov.uk/resources/ framework-for-school-inspection/ (accessed 29 January 2013).

Ofsted (2013). School Inspection Handbook (January 2013). Ref: 120101. http://www.ofsted.gov.uk/resources/school-inspection-handbook (accessed 11 February 2013).

Webber, J. (2012). 'Grade Expectations – How Comparable Outcomes Were Intended to Guarantee Fairness for Students from One Year to the Next: Where and Why This Policy Went Awry'. *Leader* 63: 14–16.

A word of thanks

Education is provided as an entitlement to all our children and young people. We have all played our part when they finally leave the premises full of confidence to whatever comes next. They often leave without the opportunity of saying thank you. Appreciation and gratitude emerge much later.

I have spent thousands of hours with children and young people and hundreds of hours with governors who give their time and expertise selflessly and with immense generosity. Pupils are often only dimly aware that governors exist at all.

When they find out they will certainly want to say *thank you*, and they would be properly puzzled if I did not take this opportunity to do so on their behalf.

To their thanks I add my own. Since first becoming a school governor in 1988, I have learnt a lot from fellow governors in the following schools: Pattishall Primary School, Towcester; Campion School, Bugbrooke; John Cleveland College, Hinckley; and Barry Primary School, Northampton. I thank you all.

Index

Praise for *The Perfect (Ofsted) School Governor*

I am delighted Tim has provided us with this brilliant little book: it may be a little book but don't be fooled. This book is mighty big in experience and wisdom – between each invaluable line of practical advice, you can be sure the words come from a practitioner who knows his stuff, who can be trusted unequivocally; who puts the child (or learner) first.

Alison Stewart, parent governor and chair

This is a book which should be in the hands of all school governors and head teachers. It would be invaluable to someone new to the role, but experienced governors and heads will find much here to guide best practice.

Tim's experience as a head teacher and consultant shines through these pages. It is unpatronising and littered with practical advice, together with nice touches of humour. The quick-start guide and glossary, together with the appendices, are very helpful, but the meat is in the book's six chapters. These cover strategic leadership, self-evaluation and policies, governors' visits to school, holding the head teacher and leadership team to account, Ofsted inspections and, last but not least, a guide to appointing a new head teacher.

Each chapter starts with a summary of what it sets out to cover and then swiftly gets down to business. In words it is economical without being too truncated and is probably best suited to being read in bite-sized chunks. There are practical suggestions for activities throughout which would help chairs and head teachers to work with the governing body to build the team and strengthen the skills and confidence of individual governors.

The narrative is particularly strong on exemplars, providing suggested formats for a range of tasks from recording meetings to planning school visits. The emphasis on getting the right questions asked in the right way is a real strength. However, this book is not just a collection of tips and suggestions: it leads and models good practice in a way that would help any governing body. It is equally applicable to primary and secondary phases and is set in the context of current models of accountability, including the Ofsted framework.

Written by an outstanding professional in his field. The strength of this book, is that the experience enshrined in it will make it relevant for a good number of years to all those concerned with supporting and challenging our schools to do their best in partnership with our children, young people and their families.

**Andrew Firman, former head teacher,
Queen's Park High School, Chester**

This is an excellent guide for all governors to review their practices and improve their performance. It will demystify the jargon for new governors and enable governing bodies to strengthen their important role in challenging and supporting the leadership of the school. It provides excellent advice on preparing for important events in the life of any school, such as appointing a new head teacher and Ofsted inspections.

**Anne Nelson, Early Years consultant,
formerly chief executive of Early Education**

This little book has plenty for everyone. There is a quick-start guide for new governors which gives an excellent introduction to the role. New governors will also find the chapter on school visits particularly useful. Equally, experienced governors will find plenty of thought-provoking material. A highlight for me is the chapter on holding the head teacher and leadership team to account. It has an excellent list of the headings under which judgements need to be reported and suggestions for questions that governors can ask. The chapter on Ofsted has a very useful 'top ten tips' for helping the school, and the chapter on appointing a new head is a must-read for governors facing this task. I can warmly recommend this book to any governor, regardless of experience. If you buy this book I can guarantee you will use it!

Crawford Craig, governor

Tim's book is a fantastic resource whether you are about to become a governor or have been involved in school governance for many years. It details what you want to know, what you should know and what you thought you knew but it turns out you didn't until now.

The chapter introductions allow you to quickly find what you're looking for, the check boxes at the end of the chapters give you something tangible to take away and work with and, because of the amount of work put into preparing the book, it feels like you're getting the advice of many educationalists and leaders in one place. You'll refer to this book for years but the first step will be reading it cover to cover.

Giles Mooney, education adviser

As a publisher and as a school governor in a local primary school, I can highly recommend this book to all school governors. This is a welcome addition to the Perfect series and an excellent and useful read – full of practical advice and governance oversight. All school governors should have their own copy.

Sonny Leong, executive chairman, Civil Service College Limited

978-178135088-1

978-178135000-3

978-178135003-4

 www.independentthinkingpress.com